PRAISE FOR EVE ESCHNER HOGAN'S *Way of the Winding Path*

"Eve Eschner Hogan has written a simple yet comprehensive guide for spiritual journeying. With easy to use activities she brings the text to life in practical terms. Eve has integrated the ancient into our modern lives with a useful tool that anyone can put into practice. You've got a great one here!"
- LUCIA CAPACCHIONE, Ph.D., A.T.R., author of *The Power of Your Other Hand* and *The Creative Journal*

"A different kind of labyrinth book. This book for the spiritual pilgrim in which the labyrinth acts as a metaphor for the path, the thread that ties it all together, and the author returns to this metaphor consistently throughout; however, unlike most books with a central focus on labyrinths, it is not even clear what kind of labyrinth she uses! And, intriguingly, that doesn't seem to make any difference. It's the path that is important, and its form appears differently to each of us."
- SIG LONEGREN, author of *Labyrinths: Ancient Myths and Modern Uses*

"A gentle yet persistent call to love sounds throughout this well-written book. Clear explanations and well-chosen illustrations invite readers to use both the labyrinth and their lives to practice spiritual devotion. Greater openness and deepening maturity await those who use this wonderful resource!"
- THE REV. JILL KIMBERLY HARTWELL GEOFFRION, PH.D., author of *Praying the Labyrinth, Living the Labyrinth, The Labyrinth and the Enneagram* and *Labyrinth and Song of Songs*.

D0017183

Way of the Winding Path

Simple Steps for
Experiencing Life
as a Spiritual Journey

Way of the Winding Path

A Map for the Labyrinth of Life

Eve Eschner Hogan

White Cloud Press
Ashland, Oregon

Printed in Canada
First White Cloud Press edition: 2003

Cover art: Stone Labyrinth and cover concept by Michael Abbey
Cover photograph by Eve Eschner Hogan
Back cover inset photograph by Wendy Kiser Eschner
Cover design by David Ruppe
Interior photos by Eve Eschner Hogan. Except p. 64, photograph © by Cindy Pavlinac
Labyrinth drawings: John Ridder, Eleven-Circuit Labyrinth, p. 8;
Jeff Saward, Seven-Circuit Universal Labyrinth, p. 8;

Library of Congress Cataloging-in-Publication Data
Hogan, Eve Eschner, 1961-
    Way of the winding path : a map for the labyrinth of life / by Eve Eschner Hogan
        p. cm.
    ISBN 978-1-883991-52-4
        1. Labyrinths--Religious aspects. 2. Spiritual life. I. Title

BL325.L3H64 2003
291.3'7--dc21

                                                                2003043081

10 03   5 4 3 2

Dedicated to Eddy, Wendy, Amy, and Emily.
No matter how many twists and turns
you find on your path through life,
may you always return to the center—to love.
Know you are loved, eternally.

Contents

PART 3: TAKING THE PILGRIMAGE HOME

Part I

THE SACRED JOURNEY BEGINS

INTRODUCTION

We can find nothing in a shrine or place of pilgrimage if we bring nothing to it, and we must never forget in the external practice of religion, that, though the Reality is everywhere, we can only make contact with it in our own hearts.
~ SWAMI PRABHAVANANDA, *How to Know God*

ONE OF THE CHALLENGES we humans have faced for eons is the belief that we must search for the sacred outside of ourselves. Pilgrimages have led us on journeys far away from home. We have looked for God from the mountaintops of the Himalayas to the peaks of Machu Pichu to the circle rounds of Stonehenge. We have searched in caves and cathedrals; we have sought out holy springs and sacred ceremonies. And, whether we know it or not, we have found the Divine in all those places—but did we really need to look so far?

Way of the Winding Path is a spiritual journey that leads us to the Divine within. Three paths entwine throughout this book: the path of the pilgrimage, the path of the labyrinth, and the path of life. Each of these metaphorically guides us to understand the others. As we peel away each layer, we reveal the Divine—no longer something we must search for. Thus, we are able to stop *seeking* and start *seeing* the blessings that surround us and the blessings that we are.

While this is not a "labyrinth book" per se, the labyrinth will be referred to throughout for the lessons it reveals for life. Whether it is a pilgrimage you make, a labyrinth you walk, or simply the life you live, *Way of the Winding Path* offers you tools for the journey. These tools include a set of skills that can be used within the context of each. You will be shown how to self-observe, align with the Divine, and take inspired action. *Way of the Winding Path* is a map to help you navigate the pathway to your own heart.

The Path of the Pilgrimage

Pilgrims are persons in motion—passing through territories not their own—seeking something we might call completion, or perhaps clarity will do as well, a goal to which only the spirit's compass points the way.
- RICHARD NIEBUHR, *Pilgrims and Pioneers*

A PILGRIMAGE is a journey to a sacred place for a devotional purpose, such as the traditional pilgrimages that thousands of people gather to take at auspicious times of the year in different places throughout the world—Jerusalem, Mecca, and Lourdes, to name just a few. But pilgrimages also refer to the personal journeys that millions of us take each day within our own lives—seeking holy teachers, retreat centers, and churches for the purpose of devotion and spiritual growth. These pilgrimages are the wonderful yet isolated moments in time in which we actively seek God. The reasons vary from person to person. Pilgrimage is an act—often a difficult one—in which we display our devotion. For some it is an opportunity to travel, to see new lands and holy places. Others make a pilgrimage to envelop themselves in the peacefulness that sacred places hold. Still others seek clarity or guidance for a problem in their lives. The key concept behind a pilgrimage is that some sort of transformation will take place—that either our lives or our very selves will be different because of the experience.

There are three primary parts to a pilgrimage:

- The first is our travel to the sacred place, which serves as preparation for reaching the destination. This is a time for us to contemplate our lives and overcome obstacles. For some, this part of the journey is made as an act of repentance, to make amends for past actions or to fulfill obligations made in bargaining with God. Some choose to journey in silence or while fasting or carrying a heavy burden. Others dance easefully down the path, celebrating their relationships with God as they go. "The journey to" offers us a time of cleansing our spirits in preparation to receive.

- The second part of the path is the time we actually spend at the sacred destination. This point often resonates with a deep peacefulness that comes from centuries of use as a place of worship and prayer. It might be the birthplace of a great master or the site of a divine event. The destination is a place to give and receive; here we make our offerings, worship, and meditate in the hope of receiving guidance for the next steps in our lives.

- The third part of the pilgrimage is the journey back home. The return trip is a time for integration, preparing us to implement the insights gained from the pilgrimage in our daily lives. The journey home is a transitional phase, bringing us back to our daily reality with new awareness and growth.

Throughout early Western history, Christians made pilgrimages to sacred places in the East to honor God and deepen their spiritual lives. But when the Crusaders roared through the Holy Land in the eleventh and twelfth centuries, the wars they ignited made it too dangerous to journey outward. At this time, the labyrinth was adapted within Western Christianity as a metaphorical pilgrimage one could take within the safety and confines of the church. The center of the labyrinth represented the sacred destination, while the walk in represented the journey to the sacred place. There is some question as to whether the medieval use of the labyrinth included the walk back out, but this portion of the journey has definitely become an important aspect for many pilgrims in the present day.

The Path of the Labyrinth

Solvitur Ambulando...It is solved by walking.
- AUGUSTINE

THE LABYRINTH referenced here specifically is the 800-year-old stonework pattern in the floor of the Chartres Cathedral near Paris, France—although variations have been found in several cathedrals throughout Europe. This same labyrinth pattern can be found in the Grace Cathedral in San Francisco; today, it shows up in many churches, parks and gardens, both public and private, throughout the world.

*Chartres Cathedral's
Eleven-Circuit Labyrinth*

The complex, eleven-circuit labyrinth found at Chartres Cathedral could easily be mistaken for a maze; at first glance, it looks like an elaborate test . . . an ancient challenge, as it were, to find the way in and out. However—unlike its sister, the maze—the labyrinth has only one path to the center; the same path brings you back out, with no dead-ends to trick or trap you along the way.

Labyrinths have been found in multiple variations on the same theme—a single, winding path to a center point, which then returns to the outside—in many different cultures, some dating back four to five thousand years. The "universal labyrinth" is simpler than the one at Chartres; typically, it has only seven circuits. In many cultures, it has also been used as a walking meditation. Labyrinths like this have a

*The Seven-Circuit
Universal Labyrinth*

8

longer history than the Chartres Cathedral labyrinth. They have been found from England to India, from South America to North America, from Greece to Scandinavia. How this exact same pattern found its way throughout the world is a bit of a mystery.

Walking the Labyrinth

JUST AS A pilgrimage outside of ourselves entails three distinct parts of the journey, so does the labyrinth walk. This three-fold path includes the walk into the labyrinth, the time spent in the center, and the journey back out.

The first part of the journey is a time for self-observation, contemplating our life circumstances and clearing the obstacles we discover as we walk. On a traditional pilgrimage, the obstacles we must overcome are usually physical and external—difficult trails, heavy loads and long distances. On the metaphorical journey within the labyrinth, the obstacles that must be cleared are internal—beliefs, perceived rules, emotions, memories, judgements, fear, grief and ego, which once surpassed, bring us to our own sacred center.

The walk in is a time of preparation, as if you are emptying your mind of thoughts, memories, expectations, and judgments, so that you are open and ready to receive guidance when you reach the center. The task is to walk the labyrinth cognizant of a "witness" state—being the observed and the observer at the same time. As you walk, simply pay attention to what you are feeling and thinking and then, with a deep breath, release it and let it go, freeing your awareness to be available for the next moment in time. As we journey the labyrinth, we encounter several 180 degree turns that represent a switch in plans, a

9

new direction, or a new set of circumstances that require us to alter our course and adjust. Often, just as we think we are nearing our goal, the labyrinthine path presents us with a plan of its own encouraging us to remain flexible and open to change.

The center of the labyrinth, the heart, represents the sacred destination. For some the center represents illumination, while others consider it a "resting place." I view it as a place of retreat, of silence, which if listened to, can be quite revealing and full of meaning. Once in the center, we are often greeted with a sense of loving gentleness as we receive insight and offer our devotion. Just as on a "real pilgrimage," here the pilgrims sit or stand in meditation open to receiving guidance. Whether you receive an answer to a question, a valuable insight about your life or merely a sense of peace, solitude or joy, the center is a quiet space in which you get what you need, if not what you came for. You come to know the stillness of the center—*your* center—as a sanctuary to which you always have access and can return whenever your soul needs rejuvenation. For most of us with busy lives our brains are working overtime—creating a lot of noise. Seldom do we retreat to silence— away from TV, radio or conversation. Having emptied all the random chatter of the brain on the way into the labyrinth, the center is a great place to be still and quiet to see what emerges. This is a journey from your head to your heart, from thought to feeling, from logic to intuition, from believing to knowing. The center of the labyrinth provides the solitude necessary for hearing the whisper of your heart—the inner voice of wisdom—as it guides you.

The journey out of the labyrinth represents Divine Alignment—returning home, in union with God, to apply in your daily life the insights and wisdom you've gained on your pilgrimage. This time is your opportunity to give thanks for the insights you received and for gathering the necessary strength and focus for taking this guidance back into the world to apply in your daily life.

While this three-fold path is a very simple and powerful model for experiencing the labyrinth, there are many ways to make meaning from the walk. Rather than a three-fold journey, some people prefer a seven-part model that includes: preparation, crossing the threshold, the journey in, time in the center, the journey out, crossing the threshold again, and integrating.[1] While others walk the labyrinth viewing it as a metaphor of the four parts of the Mass: awakening, sacrifice, transubstantiation, and culmination.[2] While I once thought there were many paths for reaching the same destination, the labyrinth has proven that there is one path and many, many ways to walk it–and to gather meaning from it.

One woman shared with me her experience taking her son to his first labyrinth walk. She carefully instructed him to walk into the labyrinth following the path and to sit down when he got to the center, which he did. She then instructed him to, "Come back out without stepping on any of the lines." So when it was time to return back out, obediently and creatively he turned and hopscotched out of the labyrinth without stepping on a single line! As you explore the labyrinth, feel free to experiment to discover your own unique way of navigating the path as it reveals personal meaning and value for you.

1. Jill Geoffrion, *Living the Labyrinth*, Pilgrim Press, 2000.
2. Sig Lonegren, *Labyrinths: Ancient Myths and Modern Uses*, Sterling, 2001

In addition to serving as a spiritual pilgrimage, labyrinths are journeyed for a multitude of other reasons. People throughout the world are rediscovering the labyrinth as a tool for clearing the mind, releasing stress and discovering solutions to life's problems. The labyrinth provides access to our inner   resources, allowing us to become more creative and resourceful in solving our problems. People have experienced emotional healing that affects their physical health simply from walking the winding path. Some have even reported they felt the presence of an ancestor or a spiritual guide as they walked.

Today, retreat centers, hospitals, schools, and churches use the labyrinth as a tool to help people feel centered and empowered.

Benefits for the Body, Mind and Spirit

EVEN IF we manage to miss the "point" of the walk, there still are benefits to the experience. Physically, the labyrinth works with the four directions and with repeated 180-degree turns. Perhaps it is some sort of "divine centrifugal force" that works on us as we walk. Somehow, mystically and magically—whether or not we are aware of any cognitive benefits, metaphors, or *ah-ha*s of awareness—the labyrinth balances our bodies, actually causing us to calm and relax, centering us.

It has been reported that researchers have taken pictures of people's auras using Kirlian photography just before they walked the labyrinth, discovering areas of blockage where the color/energy wasn't flowing. After putting these people through the labyrinth, the researchers took the photos again—and discovered that the blockages had been released and the energy was once again moving and filling in.

It is helpful to recognize that the walk itself can be every bit as beneficial physically as the *understanding* of it is beneficial mentally or spiritually. In fact, labyrinths have been found so beneficial to our health they are now being put in medical centers and hospitals. The labyrinth provides an opportunity for patients to gain a healthy perspective and peace of mind about the illness with which they are confronted. From this place of acceptance, they are better able to access their intuition and see creative options for their health.

Not only are labyrinths places for patients to go to gain balance and re-lease emotional obstacles to their health, they also are excellent tools for care-givers to get "re-centered" between patients. Labyrinths also offer a peaceful "waiting room" for anxious loved ones while family members or friends are in surgery. They provide a place for people to process their tension and concerns, and also offer arenas for nondenominational prayer, allowing family members to be of assistance in the healing. Labyrinths can also be wonderfully healing in the event of death, so much so that cemeteries, like Forest Lawn in Glendale, California, have added labyrinths to their properties so that mourners can walk through their grief.

13

The Journey is Within

AS A LABYRINTH facilitator on Maui for several years, I have shared the labyrinth experience with many locals and visiting tourists, as well as with business people during conventions. Some of these "pilgrims" came looking for spiritual experiences, some got dragged to the labyrinth walk by friends, others just stumbled upon our moonlight or sunset walks by "accident" or because they were curious. Over the past few years, I have had the very different perspective of *staying* at the "sacred destination" of the labyrinth and watching these pilgrims come and go rather than coming and going myself— and a recurring question has haunted me: How does the pilgrimage help the pilgrims, once they are safely back home?

Surely the awareness gained in the labyrinth serves us not just at the moment of insight but onward into practice and application. However, often I have found myself teaching the value of walking the labyrinth to people who do not have one in their backyards or even in their hometowns. I have wondered if I was implying that people needed to search out yet another sacred site outside of themselves (a labyrinth) in order to commune with God. In essence, I asked myself, "Am I implying that people must *take* a pilgrimage to *make* a pilgrimage?" This question has caused me to add some important elements to my labyrinth facilitation—elements that are critical to the true rhyme and reason for walking the labyrinth. Most importantly, we walk the labyrinth not as a destination but as a part of the path, as part of our life's journey. The labyrinth is a laboratory in which we can practice choosing our actions from a place of resourcefulness. The labyrinth is a map aiding us in understanding our own spiritual journey. The map, however, is not the territory. Our very lives are the territory of our sacred journeys.

Regardless of whether you have a physical labyrinth to walk, a pilgrimage to take—or whether the journey is taken within your own imagination—the important point is to bring the message of the pilgrimage home, home to your daily existence, into your life.

The Path of Life

Mystics throughout time, in all traditions, have said the same thing. We do not have to search for God, because the presence of the Divine permeates all things. If there is a search at all, it is God searching for Itself.
- RABBI DAVID COOPER, *God is a Verb*

LIFE IS A winding path that leads us this way and that. Often, we aren't even sure if we're coming or going. As in the labyrinth, just when we think we have a handle on life—just when we think we know exactly where we are and where we are going—a new event, a new character, a new idea, or a new adventure falls upon us and changes the course of our journey by 180 degrees. It's easy to lose site of our center, so to speak, when we're dealing with all the challenges life places before us. Accepting the circumstances we're presented with and handling them with grace is an opportunity that always lies before us.

Both the labyrinth and traditional pilgrimages are tools for teaching us the skills of self-observation, letting go, getting centered—aligning with the Divine, and taking inspired action. Both can magnify our opportunities to practice these skills and to listen to our intuition. However, the value is not only the isolated experience of the walk or the pilgrimage itself, it's also what we do with the insights we gain. Just as our union with God is not meant to be an isolated event from the rest of our lives, or reserved for Sundays, but

15

rather a constant state, these skills are meant to be used on a daily basis to help us. As we implement these skills in our lives, we come to see that life itself is a labyrinthine pilgrimage. By mastering the skills of self-observation, divine alignment and the magic of metaphor on the labyrinth, we are then able to transfer that mastery to life. We then recognize that rather than seeking God at some point in time or at some place in the world, or even after death, the goal of this journey is to see God—the Divine, Grace—everywhere, now.

The Three Part Journey of this Book

SIMPLY READING *Way of the Winding Path* will take you through the process of discovery. Not only is the labyrinth a tool you can use in your spiritual life right now, it also is a *metaphor* for life's sacred journey. The lessons revealed walking the labyrinth are shared here as lessons for life—for *your* life. The "walk in," Part 1 of *Way of the Winding Path*, is preparation for navigating the labyrinth of your life. You will be introduced to the tools of self-observation, letting go, and the use of metaphor, and divine alignment. When you reach the center, in Part 2, you will find eleven stories chosen to illuminate and illustrate the insights the labyrinth reveals for life. Then, as you turn out from the center, Part 3 will help you take the wisdom "home," so you can apply it every day. By doing so, you'll be empowered to achieve self-mastery.

THE MAGIC OF THE METAPHOR
The world is a mirror and life is the reflection of God.
~ SAI BABA, *Conversations with Sathya Sai Baba*

ONE OF the ways the labyrinth works is by "entrapping" the left-brain so that the right-brain is free to work with pictures and metaphors. As you may know, the left side of the brain is responsible for our linear, logical thoughts. This side of the brain is good with numbers and words. It thinks analytically and tries to make sense of things. Our right-brain, by contrast, works better with images, pictures, and metaphors. This side is more of an abstract thinker and loves to be creative. As we access this side of the brain, we are also more connected to our intuition and inner sense of knowing.

Lucia Capacchione wrote *The Power of Your Other Hand*, which is about a process she developed for writing with your non-dominant hand as a means of accessing the wisdom and creativity of your right-brain. My experience with this process was that my left-brain got so entranced trying to form the letters legibly and analyzing the process that my right-brain was free to share with me beautiful images and concepts that I didn't normally access easily. I believe walking the labyrinth works in much the same way.

As we walk the winding path, our rational minds try to figure out the rhyme and reason of the pattern. It becomes quite busy trying to stay between the lines and rationalizing the experience. I have even seen people walk the labyrinth counting the turns and paths, trying to make sense of how the pattern was formed. While our left-brain is so preoccupied, our right-brain is free to share memories, feelings, metaphors, and insights with us that we may not otherwise be free to notice.

This same phenomenon explains why we so often get great, inspirational ideas while driving down the freeway. Again, our left-brain is engaged in a task that requires its constant attention (again staying between the lines!), which allows our right-brain to flow freely. Of course, there is more to the labyrinth's secret workings than this, but this is one of the working hypotheses that my left-brain has come up with.

The labyrinth acts as a mirror or a magnifying glass, through which we capture a glimpse of our inner workings. When we use the labyrinth walk as a practice ground for learning the art of self-observation, the results can serve us tremendously because we can then apply these same skills in our daily lives.

Everything Is a Metaphor Leading Us Back to Heart

ONE OF the many ways the labyrinth teaches us is through the use of metaphor. A metaphor is a figure of speech in which a word or phrase is transferred from a situation to which it properly belongs to another, so that a comparison is implied. To use metaphor with the labyrinth, we transfer the experience or awareness that comes to us in the labyrinth walk, about the labyrinth walk, and apply it to our lives to teach us something meaningful.

For example, a friend of mine found that as he walked the labyrinth he became extremely impatient wanting to reach the center. His impatience almost caused him to give up as he endured the many twists and turns before reaching his destination. When we discussed his experience after the walk, looking at this impatience as a metaphor, he was able to transfer this awareness to see that he was also impatient in his day-to-day life, always anxious to reach his goals. With this meta-perspective or overview of his life, he was able to look at how his impatience, his need to control, was pulling him out of enjoying the present experience and interfering with his ability to focus clearly.

When I first found out about the labyrinth, I knew only of the ones at the Chartres Cathedral in France and the Grace Cathedral in San Francisco. So, I began planning to take a "pilgrimage" to San Francisco so that I could walk the labyrinth, taking a pilgrimage within. When I mentioned the labyrinth to several of my friends, I discovered that there was a labyrinth painted in the parking lot of St. John's Church on Maui, forty-five minutes from where I lived.

This was when I began learning about myself through the use of self-observation and metaphor regarding the labyrinth, because I immediately had my "spiritual attitude" mirrored back to me. I did not want to walk my sacred path in a parking lot! I had so beautifully romanticized the idea of walking the labyrinth that I actually flew 2,500 miles to San Francisco to walk it before I drove a few miles from my home for the experience.

Of course, I hadn't yet worked with the concept of metaphors, so I didn't realize what I was being shown. Instead, I took my journey to the Grace Cathedral thinking that it would be "more spiritual," rather than realizing that we can, and do, walk our sacred paths in parking lots and shopping centers, in bathrooms, at work, and every day of the week—not just on Sunday. A place or day does not need to be deemed "sacred" for us to be on our path, as *we are already on it,* all the time, even right now, wherever you may be as you read this.

I might add that these realizations don't necessarily happen at the moment of the experience. Rather, *self-observation* is necessary at the moment of the experience. In other words, you must pay attention to what you are thinking and feeling at the time, but the awareness from it may not come simultaneously. The wisdom from the experience may not come until you consider what you observed and its meaning to you—after the walk. This is why self-reflection is so important. Journaling, which I will discuss later, is a powerful tool for bringing your experience to light.

Once in San Francisco, I gathered two friends to do the walk the first time and entered the cathedral full of awe and expectation. We slipped off our shoes, set our intentions, and began the journey into the center. Enter metaphor number two: my addiction to spiritual drama. I was so full of expectations and so desirous of something spiritually dramatic, like a lightening bolt—or, rather, an enlightening bolt—that I walked the labyrinth, metaphorically speaking, with my arms so full of expectations I could not embrace anything that was offered to me.

I then was treated to my next opportunity to examine myself and the multitude of ways that I managed to get in my own way on my spiritual path. (Looking at yourself is not always fun, but it is always funny—if you are able to keep your sense of humor.) As we walked the winding path, a tourist who had traveled far to see the Grace Cathedral walked right across the labyrinth with her shoes on. My immediate reaction was full of judgment. I thought, "How dare she walk across my sacred path? What is wrong with her, doesn't she know what we are doing? And look! She has her shoes on! How disrespectful!"

With self-observation, I was able to see what I was thinking. Observing yourself is like having an uninvolved witness in your head that simply reflects back to you, without judgment, what you are doing, thinking or saying. It may sound something like this, "You are judging that lady for walking across the labyrinth," said with no intonation that implies blame, just statement of fact. With this self-awareness, we have the opportunity to learn. If we never observe ourselves, we don't have the awareness required for growth and change.

Remember, *everything is a metaphor.* The labyrinth will mirror back to the walker whatever he or she needs to see about him or herself that is getting in the way of divine alignment. By observing myself judging this woman, I was able to see that the problem was really my own need for control and approval; it was not about her at all. She had done nothing wrong. Once I let go of my judgment, I was suddenly able to see that she was merely on her own spiritual path, heading straight for the altar of the cathedral, paying no heed to anything obstructing her path. By transcending my need to control what she did and my need for others to honor me, and my path, I was able to return to my heart, my center, and honor her and appreciate her journey and my own at the same time. There is room on this planet for all of us to follow our heart paths to the Divine.

One might think that was enough self-discovery for one labyrinth walk, but no! Remember, I was still *in* the experience, observing the experience, so the lesson or awareness hadn't fully come. Instead, I was still wandering the path with great expectations of a miracle or insight worth traveling 2,500 miles for. The tension mounted as I neared the center. Surely, something extraordinary would happen there!

Just as I stepped into the center of the labyrinth, expectantly, organ music suddenly filled the cathedral. In a cathedral the size of Grace, music reverberates through the building in a very impressive way. To me, at the time, it seemed like the perfect accompaniment to emphasize my own personal melodrama. All I could do was stand in the center and laugh at myself.

I have since come to realize that when our spirituality is goal-oriented, rather than process-oriented, there can be a tremendous amount of frustration, resentment, anger and impatience that happens when we perceive we haven't reached our goal. If instead the "goal" is the process, the experience of the journey itself, then the point is to live without anger, impatience and frustration through acceptance and transcendence of the ego. Obviously, my spiritual ego was impeding my spiritual experience.

Subtle Suggestions

*The worldly man is very careful not to squander his money,
but he gives little heed to how he squanders his mind.
There is nothing greater nor easier than the constant remembrance of God.*
- SWAMI PRABHAVANANDA, *The Eternal Companion*

THE LESSONS of the labyrinth often are subtle and easily missed, if you don't witness your experience through self-observation. If I hadn't known about self-observation and metaphor, I might have entirely missed the lessons that the labyrinth provided for me. Our tendency is to walk out of the experience thinking that we learned *about the labyrinth*, rather than recognizing that we learned *about ourselves.*

One man came out of the labyrinth saying he didn't get anything out of it, that he spent the whole time trying to figure out the pattern to the design. At this point, he didn't realize that the way he analyzed or "was in his head" as he walked *was* the point—it was a form of needing control and kept him from feeling. If he took the time to look at his life, he would likely see how staying in his head is exactly what is getting in the way of his spiritual journey.

Another person walked out of the labyrinth saying, "I thought it was kind of boring. I just did it because there was nothing else to do." Again, the boredom in the labyrinth was a perfect mirror of the boredom she was creating in her life—she walked the labyrinth out of boredom in the first place. Without taking a step back and observing our experience and looking for the metaphor, gaining the awareness, we can easily miss the meaning by dismissing it at face value.

One woman came out of the labyrinth and lamented that she didn't like the fact that no one looked at her or established eye contact on the walk. She felt somewhat offended that everyone was being so "self-absorbed" and not reaching out for connection. At this point, she had a choice. She could either walk away from the labyrinth saying it is a self-centered activity, or she could look at what this feeling meant, metaphorically, *about her*. Rather than judging the labyrinth, she had an excellent opportunity to look at her needs for connection and attention (her need for approval) and to examine how that affected her daily life.

If we walk the labyrinth full of expectations, it is difficult to embrace anything we are offered along the way. Metaphorically speaking, isn't this also true in life? When we are expecting a cup of hot coffee and get a glass of cool, refreshing water instead, we are not generally pleasantly surprised. If we hadn't held the expectation of coffee, the water would have made us happy. Isn't it also true that, if we pay attention, our experience of life reveals more about us—our attitudes and beliefs, then about external events?

Reflections of Relationships

ANOTHER MODE of metaphor workings we may encounter on the labyrinth has to do with our relationships with the other walkers. Once, when introducing my husband to the labyrinth, I entered the labyrinth in front of him and immediately felt a sense of discomfort at walking in before he did. Looking at this as a metaphor, I could see that the experience paralleled an event taking place in our lives. At that time, I had a book that was about to be published and, in that moment on the labyrinth, I realized I was uncomfortable having "my projects" take off successfully before "his projects" did. Hence, my discomfort "going first." This was something I had not been aware of until revealed through metaphor. The awareness offered me the opportunity to make choices about how to handle my feelings rather than letting them sabotage my decisions without my knowledge.

Then, as we continued to walk, I was surprised to discover that while we had entered the labyrinth close together, we were immediately walking on opposite sides, seemingly a long way apart. Before I knew it, we were walking side-by-side, going in the same direction. Then, we were on opposite sides and, then again, the path amazingly brought us back together. In looking for the metaphor, I could see that our relationship was much like that. At times it seemed we were far apart, going in different directions, and other times life found us walking in the same direction side-by-side. It was comforting to view this repeating pattern within the safety of the labyrinth; it allowed me to recognize its effect on our "real" lives. I was able to see the cyclical nature of relationships and recognize that if I simply returned to center throughout times of distance, the relationship, too, would return to heart.

One of my favorite metaphorical labyrinth walks happened when I facilitated for a group of older women. We had introduced ourselves prior to walking the labyrinth and we shared our experiences afterward.

One woman said, "I realized that as I walked the labyrinth the woman named Bambi was walking in front of me. My favorite childhood character had been Bambi, so I felt like my childhood best friend walked in front of me. The woman behind me was a nurse, and my mother had been a nurse. Metaphorically, I was sandwiched, as we walked, between my childhood friend and my mother which made me feel very safe. Then, several times when I came around a turn, I came face to face with the woman who had shared that she was a widow. My greatest fear in life is becoming a widow, and there was my fear, confronting me repeatedly."

The woman then stopped her sharing for a moment to ask, "What was the woman's name who left the walk early?" referring to a woman who had walked off the labyrinth right in the middle of the walk because her ride had

25

come to pick her up. We told her that the name of the woman who had left early was Pat.

With that piece of information she gasped and said, "My daughter's name was Pat, and she died young!" It seems that somehow the labyrinth mirrored back to her these important relationships in her life, pieces of her life puzzle, so she could examine them from a different perspective.

The labyrinth works with subtleties that are not always so obvious. If we can simply observe our experiences and spend a moment reflecting on the awareness we've gained, insights will emerge that allow us to make simple shifts in the way we are living so as to better align our thoughts and actions with our most divine selves.

EXPANDING THE BOUNDARY

It is possible to pray at all times, in all circumstances and in every place and easily to rise from frequent vocal prayer to prayer of the mind, and from that to prayer of the heart, which opens the kingdom of God within us.
~ ST. JOHN CHRYSOSTOM

THE IMPORTANT message for us as pilgrims on our spiritual path is not that we must have a labyrinth in order to experience God—or our sacred path; rather, the labyrinth is a wonderful tool within which to *practice* hearing God or experiencing the sacred journey. After using the labyrinth as a "laboratory" for practicing the skills of self-observation, gaining awareness, letting go, getting centered, and taking action from the heart, then we are in the position of being able to expand the boundary of the labyrinth to use these skills all the time.

The point of looking at metaphors is that what we experience on the labyrinth is seldom about the labyrinth experience itself but, rather, about something else in our lives we are invited to see. While in the "lab" (labyrinth/laboratory), we can master the art of recognizing that our thoughts and judgments about others are not really about them, but are opportunities for us to look at ourselves and our desire to love. Our judgments *about others* have little to do with those whom we judge and everything to do with our need to love—which, if observed, can be released, allowing us to return to being loving. Our fear of judgment *from others* is really about our desire to be loved. Once released, we can return to heart and move forward on our path in union with the Divine. When we let go of the *need* to be loved and to love, we find that we truly *are* loving and loved. Love is our true nature, and the *need* for love is an ego-based fear that we are not already so. Once we remove that obstacle, we are able to settle into our hearts, into our center, and simply *be* the love that we are. When we let go of the obstacles, love fills the void.

Everything we encounter on the path is really a metaphor to mirror to us what we need to see to bring us closer to the Divine, closer to love, closer to our hearts. The labyrinth acts as a magnifying glass to help us with this process; but if we don't have a labyrinth at our disposal, we can still achieve the necessary awareness to master these skills. Gaining this mindset requires that we practice self-awareness by setting our intention. We can begin by looking at our everyday lives through a "labyrinthine" filter. Every encounter with others is an opportunity to look at ourselves, to observe ourselves, to let go of the obstacles between us and love.

In actuality, the labyrinth design itself is a metaphor of our spiritual journey. Where does the boundary of the labyrinth, our sacred path, actually begin? At the edge of a forty-foot circle? What if the three-fold pilgrimage of your sacred path actually begins when you leave home on your journey to a labyrinth, the sacred destination is your time on the labyrinth, and your journey completes when you return back home the way you came?

What if, for those going on a pilgrimage, the sacred journey begins when they fly across the globe to the sacred center—Jerusalem, Lourdes, the Himalayas, Mecca, Chartres—and then completes as they fly back home the way they came? Where does the sacred journey begin?

What if we expand the boundary of the labyrinth even further to recognize that our sacred journey begins with the process of birth, and that we spend our lives in the sacred center of life on this heavenly planet and then we return back out through death?

What if the boundary is even larger than that? What if we were to live our lives as if we were always on a pilgrimage—on a journey toward the Divine, with the Divine, as the Divine? We are already on the path. We are on a pilgrimage; life is a pilgrimage! Our sacred journey has already begun, and we are always on it, as the Divine presence is always with us—whether we are in a shopping center parking lot, stuck in traffic, praying in a church, or sitting in meditation on a mountaintop in Tibet. All of our daily encounters are metaphors to bring us closer to the Divine. We just need to raise our awareness, to expand the boundary, so that we can see our lives from this perspective.

A man at a sunset labyrinth walk recently shared that he had been actively seeking his spiritual path, but was disappointed he hadn't found it yet. I gently reminded him that he was already on it, and was now merely trying to make sense of it.

So, how can you make sense of it? The following pages will describe to you how to achieve divine alignment through self-observation and letting go—tools that will guide you on your path through life. If you have a labyrinth to practice these skills on, wonderful. If not, rest assured that your life serves equally well as practice ground! Imagine, if we expanded the labyrinth to include our very lives and applied these skills every day, how different our lives would be!

DIVINE ALIGNMENT

Where reverence is, pride will not come.
The source of honor is divinity in you.
The source of reverence is divinity in others.
- SWAMI SASTRANANDA

ORIGINALLY, I got interested in the labyrinth not as an experience in and of itself but because I saw it as the perfect experiential tool for understanding the concepts I was teaching in my personal growth and relationship seminars. These workshops revolve around helping participants access their inner resources and enhance their self-esteem, which I define as "knowing our own Divine essence *and* living in alignment with that knowing."

Someone once heard me say this and asked, "What do you mean by 'Divine'?"

To which I replied, "God."

She then asked, "Whose God?"

In response to the implication that there is more than one God, I replied, "Ours."

Spirituality is about transcending the ego. Religion, on the other hand, is based on, even dependent upon, ego—"my God," "my religion," "my way." Religion serves a very important role, but our spirituality should not stop there. It needs to go beyond religion, beyond Sunday, beyond the church, beyond names and forms, into our very core. In order to know the Divine, it doesn't matter what you chose to call God, or what form of God you choose to worship. So if my words are getting in your way, simply substitute your words in their place. If "the Christ within" or the "Golden Buddha Within" or "Higher Power" work better for you, simply change the words as you read. The meaning will remain the same.

This "divine essence" I refer to is simply, love. We are here to love and be loved—we are love. Any time we are not operating from love, we are out of alignment.

Divine alignment requires five steps that can be practiced and applied in any given moment. Step one is *Self-Remembrance*, step two is *Self-Observation*, step three is *Letting Go*, step four is *Getting Centered* and step five is *Taking Aligned Action*. With practice, it only takes a split second to achieve all five steps.

In order to begin the process of transformation, to raise our self-esteem and align with our core essence, we must "wake up" and remember that *we are spiritual beings*. Essentially, the labyrinth offers *experiential spirituality*—an opportunity to *experience* ourselves as spiritual beings rather than just being *told* that we are. After facilitating a labyrinth walk at the beautiful Rancho La Puerta Spa in Tecate, Mexico, a woman emerged from the labyrinth, looked up at me and said, "Wow. Where have I been all my life?"

For many people, it's hard to imagine that we have a divine core. Just like the twisting, winding labyrinthine path that revolves around the still center, our lives may be in such chaos that we have deeply forgotten this aspect of our being and no longer know it exists. For others, you may have been raised to think that there is no divine core within, only a "sinner." But this divine essence *does* exist, and we have all had glimpses of it or moments of spiritual awareness—we just don't always recognize it.

Sometimes this awareness takes the form of a peaceful recognition of a connection to a greater whole, other times it materializes as what I lovingly refer to as "spiritual indigestion." This is when a feeling surges to the surface and gnaws at us for attention, reminding us that there is more to life than meets the eye, that there is a divine order or rhyme and reason to things.

Recently, at a labyrinth walk I held for high school students, one young man was practically jumping up and down with excitement as he emerged from the labyrinth. Afterwards, we asked him about his experience. He enthusiastically shared, amazed by his own realization, "I discovered that I have a happy soul! Underneath my anger, frustration and stress, underneath it all, my soul is happy! I am really happy!"

This knowledge, this recognition that at our core, our center, we all have a "Happy Soul" is the knowing with which we are aiming to align. When we know our own divine essence and live in alignment with that knowing, we experience ourselves as powerful, joyful and capable beings—and are able to honor others as such, as well. When we are living in divine alignment, life becomes a magical, wonder-filled, mysterious journey.

Magical Moments

If we could see the miracle of a single flower clearly, our whole life would change.
- JACK KORNfiELD, Buddha's Little Instruction Book

SOMETIMES THIS remembrance occurs as a magical moment, when something happens that causes us to stop and feel a sense of awe. It often is as simple as a moment when something so "coincidental" happens that you have to pause to wonder. It may occur as a moment of clarity, a startling realization, or a brief encounter that carries an emotional impact or has a recognizable importance, even if you don't understand it—like a dream you'll never forget.

Sudden memories or déjà vu experiences—when you feel as if you are encountering something for the second time when, as far as you know, it is only your first —also are magical "reminder" moments. Most of us have had one of these memorable moments when we have met someone new and felt an instant rapport, sure that we knew them already.

Magical moments are the ones that cause you to silently give thanks; quite often they happen when we are out in nature. These experiences can be anything from seeing a butterfly gliding in a whole new light to getting a parking spot in a crowded lot, from watching a flower bloom to seeing the birth of a new life, from sharing a moment with a wild animal to looking into the eyes of a beloved. It might be sitting under a large tree feeling peaceful to your depths, or come in an impassioned moment of creativity and artistic expression. It also might come in the form of sudden understanding—when you realize why something happened to you that at the time seemed tragic, but now you can see how the experience changed you for the better, or how your life path was enhanced because of it.

These are the moments when you realize that a coincidence is more than it seems. Squire Rushnell, author of *When God Winks*, says, "Coincidence—God winks—are little messages to you on your journey through life, nudging you along the grand path that has been designed especially for you." Dr. Gerald Jampolsky calls a coincidence "a miracle in which God wishes to stay anonymous." Look to those moments that nag at your soul to wake up—and pay attention!

Remembering who we are also happens through heart connections with others. By recognizing the signs of someone else's divine nature, we are better able to see those same signs within ourselves. Often when we observe children living so authentically, the absolute wonder and joy of life is mirrored back to us, reminding us of who we are.

Once we start paying attention to the magical moments in our lives, it is possible to begin seeing that *every* moment is magical, not just the monumental, obvious moments. We can shift into a constant state of awe and appreciation, recognizing everything as divine creation and seeing ourselves as such. In this state, we recognize all experiences and encounters, even painful ones, as perfect blessings to lead us closer to our hearts. Practice and intention are all that are necessary for this shift to take place.

Resetting Our "Zeros"

If you let cloudy water settle, it will become clear.
If you let your upset mind settle, your course will also become clear.
- JACK KORNFIELD, *Buddha's Little Instruction Book*

MEDITATION IS another means of accessing this centered, connected place within. For most of us, when meditating in the traditional sense, we find it very difficult to still our thoughts and quiet our minds—especially at first. The labyrinth walk can be very helpful with overcoming this challenge as the practice we gain calming the mind while walking is easily transferred to meditation while sitting. Because the labyrinth walk is a walking meditation, it leads pilgrims to the center, not only physically, but to their center spiritually, so they can feel their own peaceful, loving essence. Once experienced and identified, we are then able to recognize the influence and presence of that divine center all the time. Access has been granted and the refuge is there, for the taking.

Meditation, walking or sitting, is a great way to "reset your zeros." Consider your bathroom scale and how it periodically needs to be reset to zero in order to give you an accurate weight. If you neglect to do this, over time, slowly but surely, the scale will get further and further out of balance until it is totally inaccurate. If you never do it in the first place, the scale will always be off, giving you inaccurate feedback. The same is true for people. If we spend even just a few moments every day in silence, reaffirming our spiritual journey and relationship with God, we "reset our zeros" in a state of peace, strength and wisdom. Every day that we miss this practice, we get a little further from center, a little further out of balance, until we forget entirely that we have a happy, peaceful source within. Suddenly, we find ourselves unable to cope and our lives in turmoil and chaos. It is said that Gandhi meditated two hours a day, except when things were really demanding and busy, on those days he meditated for four!

In the book, *How to Know God*, Swami Prabhavananda explains, "If the body is thought of as a busy and noisy city, then we can imagine that, in the middle of this city, there is a little shrine, and that, within this shrine, the Atman, our real nature, is present. No matter what is going on in the streets outside, we can always enter that shrine and worship. It is always open." Find a moment or two every day to reflect, reconnect, give thanks for the magical moments and enter the shrine within.

Self-Observation

In the name of God, stop a moment, close your work, look around you.
- LEO TOLSTOY

ONCE WE become aware of this self-remembrance, the next step is to begin aligning our outer worlds with our inner knowing. You begin by making a self-assessment through self-observation. Take a look at yourself and assess exactly "where you are now" on your map of life. Self-observation leads to self-awareness. Through awareness we recognize that we have choice. When we have choice, we are empowered. As powerful beings we realize that we are responsible for the experiences we create and the quality of our lives. Our experiences on this journey of life are up to us!

THE SACRED JOURNEY BEGINS

Just like taking a road trip, decide where you want to go, then look at your surroundings to determine where you already are. From there you can adjust your direction to align with your goal. This divine alignment is a state of being centered, balanced, and one with your Higher Self. This is when you are identifying with your strong, all-knowing, wise essence—your center, rather than with your weak, scared, reactionary self—the twists and turns.

The art of self-observation is that of becoming a witness, an observer of your life, while at the same time remaining a participant. Several times each day, practice by simply asking yourself, "What am I doing now? How am I feeling now?" By recognizing that part of you that is the witness, the observer, you realize that this very same part is not involved in the drama of your life, but merely watching and guiding you—*when you choose to listen.* The more you practice, the more easily you will be able to identify and access this inner wisdom.

Consider the pattern of the labyrinth itself. The twisting, turning, often confusing path winds around a peaceful, calm, ever-present center. The winding path leads us through a series of 180-degree turns. We may experience anxiety, wondering where the path will take us next and whether we are going the right way. We encounter others as we journey—some with whom we feel rapport and others from whom we feel totally disconnected. Sound familiar? The journey of life unfolds before us, and yet there is a still, calm, unwavering center in the midst of the winding path. As we walk the pathway, it helps to remember that we can draw from the strength and peacefulness this core provides. This is also true of ourselves—we each have a still calm center within, regardless of the drama around us.

37

Our spirit, our true essence, is not caught up in the soap opera lives that surround us. This aspect of our being is still, calm, and strong in the midst of adversity. Identifying with this part of ourselves is always a matter of choice. Unfortunately, few of us ever take the time to tap into that source-well, opting instead to become reactive to everything that goes on around us.

I remember once sobbing on my living room couch after breaking up with a long-term boyfriend. As I sat there gasping for breaths between the tears, I heard a voice in my head make a simple statement of observation: "Listen to that! You are really crying. You haven't cried like this in years." Even though I was completely caught up in expressing my emotions, I could feel the part of me that was not at all involved in the pain of breaking up with my boyfriend. The "observer" simply remained calm, strong, non-judgmental and wise. I realized then that I could choose to identify with *that* aspect of my being, rather than buying into the drama and pain I was creating. I could choose to identify with the part of me that could see the big picture, the whole journey, rather than just one turn in the path.

Walking the labyrinth offers a practice ground to isolate and identify the voice of wisdom within. Once you come to know the voice of your Higher Self, you can separate it from the other tapes that are playing in your head and stay centered instead of buying into the stream of chatter that bombards you. As your thoughts, feelings and memories emerge on your labyrinth walk, if you simply observe them, acknowledge their presence and then release them, you won't get caught in the drama. Rather than walking the rest of the path plotting, planning or analyzing whatever topic that pops into your head, observe it, let it stay just a moment and then let it go. As you become skilled at this within the labyrinth, you can then manage your emotions in much the same way in your daily life.

As a means of example, imagine that you are the sky. You know you are the sky, yet you have clouds that pass through from time to time. Rather than *becoming* the clouds and getting carried away, simply *observe* the clouds, knowing that you are *not* the clouds. Rather than saying, "I am a cloud," say instead, "Hmmm, look at all these clouds." From there, you are able to choose what to do about the clouds—let them gather to shower the landscape with rain, or create a wind that dissipates them. By practicing self-observation, you can recognize your feelings and allow them to pass by without getting caught up in them—without *becoming* them.

This is not to suggest that you should *suppress* the feelings that come up but, rather, that you *transcend* them. When you become the observer, you realize that you have feelings, *but you are not the feelings*. You can *feel* anger or sadness without *being* anger or sadness. So often when people experience a traumatic event, they identify with and become their grief instead of recognizing it as a passing storm. It is from this state that they begin to think this situation or this feeling will never pass and hopelessness sets in. But, of course, our emotions are fluid and ever changing, they are not static.

As a counselor of teenagers, I had a student come in and tell me about how joyful and ecstatic she was about a new love. She was on "cloud nine," and could not possibly be happier. A few days later, she returned to my office feeling suicidal because of something that happened over the weekend; she thought

39

her misery would never pass. I reminded her how quickly things changed for the worse, and how quickly things could change again for the better. It is all a divine play. *Shift* happens! Our opportunity is to be the observer and watch what we are offered from a place of knowing that *we are not the drama;* instead, we can determine what we want to do about it. The path in the labyrinth, as in life, will turn us in the opposite direction than we were going, but we must remain fluid, as the path is guaranteed to turn us again—and again.

Self-observation also allows us to witness our self-talk—the words we say to ourselves, and the feelings that emerge as a result. Our feelings are a direct result of our thoughts. When we observe our thoughts, we become aware of the effect that we have on ourselves. Once we are aware, we begin to recognize that we have choice. We can choose the words we say to ourselves. By choosing different words and different thoughts, we can create different feelings. At the very least, we can choose what it is that we decide to honor. A misunderstanding many people have is thinking that they have to turn their doubting minds off and completely stop the tape of self-criticism they may have carried with them since childhood in order to experience peace. It is a matter of choice, not elimination.

Even after years and years of self-esteem work, I will be presenting to a group of people and I still get that voice in the back of my mind that says things like, "That person doesn't like you. That was a stupid thing to say. Tsk, Tsk, you said 'um' again." Judgmental commentary such as this is not the voice of a wise observer, rather it is the voice of an inner critic. The key isn't trying

40

to get rid of that voice, rather it is *not identifying* with that voice or the things it says. While none of this commentary is something I want to hear, if I listen to it from a place of self-observation and identification with my Higher Self, I don't have to buy into it. I have a choice whether or not to *honor* "the voice."

Instead, from a witness state, I can simply observe without getting paralyzed by what is being said. Instead of thinking, "I knew it, I am no good!" I simply observe and think, "Oh, there's that tape again," without automatically believing everything it says. From this perspective, the things that are said are actually pretty funny. At worst, I will be entertained; at best, I will learn something about myself and receive useful information I can use. A great saint said, "If someone speaks ill of you, first see if he is right. If he is right, try to correct yourself. If it is unjust, then forget." The same holds true for our constant self-assessments.

Learning to recognize the "voice of wisdom" and the "voice of the critic" so that you can tell them apart is one of the benefits of self-observation. A clue as to the difference is that the voice of wisdom will empower you, making you feel stronger. The voice of the critic will result in feeling weak, less capable and more dependent on outside sources of strength. Self-esteem is knowing our divine essence, our higher self, and taking action in alignment with that knowing.

41

When we are in a state of divine alignment, we are our most resourceful selves and most capable of making healthy decisions, because we see all of our options. In this state of alignment, we have access to our intuition—and, more importantly, we trust it. It is helpful to recognize that initially this state of esteem or alignment generally is not a constant state. It requires many "return visits" before it becomes habitual. Although we were born with all the qualities we need to access and live in alignment with this state of being, we have learned many habits and ways of being that get in our way. Our opportunity now is to remove those obstacles and access our true essence to live conscious, proactive, joyful, and purposeful lives. For this, self-observation is a critical, continuously repeated, step.

Removing the Obstacles

Your task is not to seek for love,
but to find the barriers in yourself that you have built against it.

COURSE IN MIRACLES

THERE IS really one primary obstacle to love from which all other apparent obstacles stem. This obstacle is the ego. The ego causes us to judge. The ego causes us to fear. The ego causes us to blame. The ego causes us to fight. When we learn to recognize the ego at work, to observe it rather than to become it, we can learn to transcend the ego and return to love. Self-observation allows us the opportunity to look at ourselves, see the ego in action, remember our divine essence, return to that loving essence, and then take aligned action.

Ego presents itself as two obstacles to divine alignment: the *need* to love and the *need* to be loved, which translate dysfunctionally as a need for control and a need for approval. These obstacles may manifest in a variety of ways—anger, hurt, fear, judgement, low self-esteem, codependence, anxiety, etc. However, these are just the symptoms that can be tracked back to one or both of these core obstacles.

Remember, our true essence *is* love. The problem here isn't the love, but rather the *need* to love and be loved. While our souls *are* love, our egos misconstrue this and interpret love as an ego need, instead of just who we are. The ego thinks that in order to love, it must approve of someone else. In order to approve of someone else, they must behave the way we want them to. In order to get them to behave the way we want them to, we must control them. Suddenly, our soul's desire to be itself—love, is suddenly showing up as a need to control others. Likewise, the ego thinks that in order to be loved, it must be accepted and receive approval from others, thus being loved suddenly turns into a need for approval.

When we operate from these needs, rather than from being love, we are actually blocking our heart energy of love and compassion; thus, decisions made in the midst of these needs will not be resourceful (re-source-ful—once again, full of Source). These ego needs are based in the head, which is why the journey from head to heart is so important. When we are "in our heads," we are generally cut off from our hearts. When we are in our hearts, however, we are able to use our heads. Once we release these obstacles, we free ourselves to truly give and receive love. The idea here is to grow who you really are, while letting go of who you really aren't.

The labyrinth is an excellent tool for discovering these obstacles and releasing them. However, the process of discovery is the same whether you are in the labyrinth or in your daily life. To discover these influences working on you, you must be self-observant as you walk. Be the walker on the path while at the same time witnessing yourself as you walk. If, while walking the winding path, you find yourself wanting to throw your arms up toward the heavens as a gesture of the gratefulness you are experiencing, but you stop yourself because you think, "What will people think of me? Will they think I am just being dramatic?" This is a perfect opportunity to observe yourself and recognize that this blockage of your experience is about your need to be loved, to be approved of. This very concern has stopped the flow of love to and from your heart and has stopped your expression of joy making you less lovable because you are now being inauthentic. At the moment of that awareness, all you need to do is simply take a few deep breaths and "breathe out" that need, releasing it. Then, return to your heart and determine whether or not it is truly your heart's desire to hold your arms up to the sky and, if so, take the action from there—in divine alignment. By returning to your heart and choosing an inspired action, you open yourself to actually receive love, rather than needing it. Any time you find yourself worrying about what others are thinking of you, or altering your heart's desire in order to receive the approval of others, you are actually blocking your ability to be loved.

44

Or, if while walking the winding path, you see someone else throw her arms up toward the heavens as a gesture of the gratefulness she is experiencing, and you think, "Who does that person think she is, being so dramatic?" You are having the golden opportunity to see in yourself the need to control, to approve of others. At the moment of this awareness, simply breathe out this need, return to your heart, your center, and allow others their own experiences on this sacred path. In the moment of self-observation, we become aware of our choices. We have a choice to stay stuck in fear and judgment or to move out of it, returning to love, to heart, to center. Anytime you find yourself judging others or trying to control their behavior, you are actually blocking your ability to love. Remember, there are many ways to walk the path!

The labyrinth is a perfect experiential tool for practicing the art of self-observation, letting go of the inner obstacles we encounter, getting centered and resourceful, and then taking action from that place of clarity. You will find that your needs for approval and control are mirrored to you within the labyrinth; you can then use that observation to show you what you need to let go of outside of the labyrinth to bring you back to your heart in your daily life.

While the labyrinth is a great practice ground for self-discovery, once the discovery is made, you can use this knowledge to transform every moment. Any time that you find yourself feeling a conflict—whether internal or with someone else—stop, self-observe, and identify whether it is your need for control or approval that is getting in your way. Simply, remember who you really are, take a deep breath—or two or three—and release the need, which will allow to you to return to center. From there you can choose the appropriate, aligned action. [3]

---

3. For more information on living resourcefully and the process of letting go, read *Rings of Truth* by Jim Britt, with Eve Eschner Hogan (Health Communications Inc.: 1999).

It is interesting to note that the need for approval and the need for control are really just opposite sides of the same ego-coin. The more work you do on observing, identifying and releasing them, the more similar they will seem to you. As, in reality, it all boils down to our desire to be what we really are—love—and that which blocks love—ego.

The more you work with this concept the more you will also realize that what you experience has very little, if anything to do with what is going on_*outside* of you and almost entirely is a result of what is going on *inside* of you. One of author Don Miguel Ruiz's four agreements from his book by the same title is "Don't take anything personally." I would add to that, "Don't take anything personally *that anyone else does, and take everything personally that you do!*" Likewise, everything you notice outside of yourself is metaphorical of your spiritual journey. Everything you notice inside of yourself is a result of choice.

Part 2

Lessons from the Labyrinth

A Three-Fold Path
Preparation: Sections 1–5
Illumination: Section 6
Divine Alignment: Sections 7–11

1.
REMEMBER WHO YOU ARE

When the lake of the mind becomes clear and still,
man knows himself as he really is, always was and always will be.
- SWAMI PRABHAVANANDA, *How to Know God*

ONE OF MY favorite metaphors came to me as I learned to scuba dive. Floating on the ocean, you are subject to the turbulence of the sea. You can be tossed to and fro by the waves, or blasted by wind and rain. However, once you drop below the surface, everything changes. You are suddenly—within just a few feet—immersed in tranquility. The water becomes calm.

From this vantage point, you can look up and see the boat being thrown around and see the waves splashing above you without being a part of it. You become the observer of the chaos, rather than its victim.

The metaphor of walking the labyrinth is much like this. As you walk the labyrinth, notice that no matter which way you turn, no matter how confused you may become on the path, the sacred center is always there. It remains unwavering, clear, calm, right there within your reach all the time. It calls out to you; it pulls you toward it, always accessible. Once you have reached the center, you can look out upon the trail you have journeyed to see all the twists and turns, yet remain apart from that chaos.

We also have a sacred center, a divine core of strength and wisdom accessible to us at all times. Remembering this is the first and most important step toward transformation—for, without this knowing, this self-remembrance, there is nothing for us to align our thoughts and actions with. It is a divine anchor, if you will.

⊕ Take a moment, several times a day, to simply stop and become self-aware. Whenever you feel uneasy or "off center," take a moment to step back and self-remember. Remember yourself to be a spiritual being; realign your thoughts, feelings, and actions with your Highest Self.

⊕ Periodically through the day, repeat the words, "I am," reminding yourself that the "I" is your spirit—not your ego—and that your divine essence does, indeed, exist. Then extend this as you encounter others to "I am you. I am you."

2.
SELF-OBSERVE

To acquire knowledge, one must study; but to acquire wisdom, one must observe.
~ MARILYN VON SAVANT

ON THE LABYRINTH there have been times when I have gotten distracted for a moment and, when I returned to the task at hand (walking to center), I wasn't sure if I had gotten turned around and was heading in the wrong direction. By taking a moment to self-observe, "Where am I now?"—and even looking ahead of me a little ways, asking, "If I continue in the direction I am heading, where will it lead me?" while remembering my intention, "I am a spiritual being on a sacred path"—I have been able to realign with my goals, realign with my purpose, and confidently continue on my spiritual journey.

Self-observation and self-remembrance are the very first steps on an inward journey. Self-observation allows us to make conscious choices rather than act and react from an "automatic pilot." With self-remembrance—remembering our own true essence—our choices will be in divine alignment. It acts as a divine compass.

What this means in practice is that in any given moment we can take a mental snapshot of what we are doing and how we are feeling and compare that snapshot with the inner picture we have of our own divine essence. If what we are doing or what we are feeling does not appear to be in alignment with the essence that we are, we can make a new choice to align the two by choosing new actions, thoughts, feelings, and words.

⊕ Continuously, throughout the day, ask yourself these questions, "Where am I now?" "What am I doing now?" "How am I feeling now?"

⊕ Observe yourself for the answers, remember who you are, realign with your heart, and continue on from there.

3.

APPRECIATE THE JOURNEY

As you walk and eat and travel, be where you are.
Otherwise you will miss most of your life.
- JACK KORNFIELD, *Buddha's Little Instruction Book*

WHEN I WAS eighteen, I went backpacking on Kauai along the magnificent Na Pali Coast. This trail follows the coastline, weaving in and out of ravines and valleys. As I hiked the winding path, at every lookout point I would set my sights on the goal, Kalalau Valley—the sacred destination eleven miles in the future.

Once I arrived, I spent three days enjoying the magic of my destination and then opted to take a boat ride back out. From the boat, I was treated to seeing my journey from a different perspective. I was surprised to see what an incredibly beautiful eleven miles I had passed through—cascading waterfalls, lush greenery, and long-tailed Tropic birds. I had missed all of this splendor on the way because I spent the entire walk looking toward my destination, thinking about how much further until I was there, and counting the miles.

If we take a moment to consider our lives, we can easily see how much we miss by staying so focused on where we are going rather than on where we are. By focusing on what we want, rather than what we already have, we miss the everyday joys of life.

Sometimes, I continue to find myself to be very goal-oriented and forward-focused, concerning myself greatly with where I am going and what I am "supposed" to be doing with my life. The labyrinth mirrored this "obsession" to me, as I walked it with the same kind of focus on "getting there," anxious to arrive at the center.

When I observed myself, I realized that I wanted the approval of doing it "right" and the control of knowing where I was going, which left me feeling unbalanced and fearful that I was doing life "wrong." My fears pulled me out of the present moment, taking away the enjoyment of my journey.

In an inspired moment on the labyrinth, I turned around and walked the entire way out of the labyrinth backwards. What I discovered as I walked backwards was that I didn't ever need to look "where I was going" to reach the desired outcome. All I truly needed to do was pay close attention to where I was in the moment and to self-adjust when I stepped "out of line." I then set my sights on enjoying the journey rather than focusing on the results. By offering thanks for every turn in the path, every new perspective and experience, I was able to see that it all was a blessing. The journey, while different, is just as sacred as the destination.

⊕ Remember to enjoy the journey and appreciate every moment.

⊕ Life does not "begin" when you get "there"—it doesn't start when you graduate from school, or when you get married, or when you have kids, or when you get divorced.

⊕ Life is here and now.

⊕ Our sacred path is not a destination, it is a process.

⊕ Enjoy! Give thanks!

4.
LET GO

When the 'I' is not, the real 'I' opens.
- OSHO, The Book of Secrets

OFTEN, WHEN I facilitate a labyrinth walk, I am faced with my own pre-conceived notions of how the walk should go or with concerns about how I am doing as a facilitator. The walkers also experience these hesitations, wondering, *What will people think about me as I walk? Am I walking too slow or too fast? Am I "getting it?"*

At times like these, the labyrinth is showing us our ego-needs to love and be loved. When we take the time to self-observe, allowing a glance toward the center to remind us of the still, calm center within us, we can easily let go of these needs, knowing that when we are centered and resourceful, we *are* love, we *have* love, and we are able to *give* love. We don't *need* what we *already have.*

When you discover one of these ego-needs impeding your progress toward your heart, take several deep breaths and breathe them out as if you are breathing out a cloudy smoke veil that's been blocking your essence. With each breath, see yourself lighter and shinier. Return to resourcefulness and continue your life journey from there.

Self-observation is illuminating. When we turn on a light in a dark and scary room, we are able to see the true nature of the shapes that scared us and we no longer feel the fear. The "snake" is revealed as a coil of rope and the "boogie man" as just a chair. When we witness ourselves, we turn on the light of awareness. Then we are able to transcend our fears and illusions and align with our true natures.

As I enter the labyrinth, sometimes I pretend that I am carrying along a large bag full of the past: past experiences, past limitations, past pains, past beliefs, past emotions, and past loves. As I walk into the center, with each step and each breath, I mentally reach into the bag and pull out a piece of the past and let it go. I release it with an offering of acceptance and appreciation for its part in my life—not as a rejection. I imagine that as I release each piece, it turns into a bird or butterfly and flies away. It is happy to be free, and I become lighter and lighter and freer, as well. By the time I reach the center, by releasing the past, I have prepared myself to be in the present, to be in the Presence. I am now ready to embrace what *is*, rather than carry what *was*.

⊕ When you feel that something is off, stop, self-remember, self-observe, and release the obstacles that are pulling you out of the present moment, out of divine alignment.

⊕ By reconnecting with your center, you are free to choose your actions—actions that align with your goals and your sacred core.

5.
TRUST THE PROCESS

After you have sown in the soil of Cosmic Consciousness your prayer-seed,
do not pluck it out frequently to see whether it has germinated.
Give the divine forces a chance to work uninterruptedly.
- PARAMAHANSA YOGANANDA, Scientific Healing Affirmations

I WAS ASKED to facilitate a labyrinth walk with a group of people who were on Maui as an incentive trip, because they were this company's best sales people, nationwide. I agreed, thinking that these men and women had been told what we would be doing and so were prepared for the experience.

When I arrived, however, I was told that they had decided to provide the labyrinth experience as a surprise and that none of the participants knew anything about it. This wasn't much of a problem, although I was a bit concerned that they might not be open to it, coming unaware, from varying backgrounds.

Next, while setting up, I was told that the participants had been at dinner—with an unending supply of wine. This concerned me a bit more, as I began to doubt the labyrinth's effectiveness with people totally unprepared, unsuspecting, and under the influence of alcohol. Having had people in the past say that the labyrinth made them dizzy, I tried to envision this group walking the winding path already tipsy and my apprehension grew.

Remembering that the labyrinth experience is *always* a metaphor, even for me as a facilitator, I knew that my concerns were really about *me*, not about the *participants*, and that I was being provided an opportunity to release my own needs for control and approval. I took a deep breath as the group entered the room, and I shared the labyrinth from my heart, trusting that the experience would be perfect.

What started as my scariest group quickly became one of the best. Making a joke of walking the sacred path under the influence of alcohol, we all laughed as I told them how to get the most out of the experience. Then, as we approached the labyrinth, the group became quite reverent, maintaining silence from the beginning prayer. I watched the group, dressed in beautiful, floral aloha wear, as they wove their way in and out of the labyrinth, reminding me of a maypole dance. When they emerged from the labyrinth, they all had stories to tell of the impact of the experience.

The moral of the story for me was to trust the labyrinth, trust the process, and trust myself, knowing that even if "they" hadn't "gotten it," the experience would have been perfect anyway.

When things appear to be going wrong or not the way we have planned, we easily get pulled out of the present moment and become fearful of what might happen. We often want to control circumstances that are not within our control. By staying centered, we are able to see our options and tap into our creativity to find perfect solutions.

⊕ Do you let fear paralyze you during the course of your day?

⊕ Practice "trusting the process." Hold within yourself a deep knowing that when you are in your heart, you can use your head.

⊕ Choose to trust that everything is perfect, everything has a reason, even if it doesn't seem so. Look for evidence of this perfection, and surely you will be able to see the "silver lining" to any experience—maybe not right away, but eventually.

6.
LISTEN TO THE VOICE OF GOD

If we really want to pray, we must first learn to listen;
for in the silence of the heart God speaks.
- MOTHER TERESA, Everything Starts from Prayer

I WAS CALLED to facilitate a labyrinth walk for a youth group in Lahaina, Maui. When I arrived to set up the labyrinth, the Tongan community was holding their weekly service in the church, so we were serenaded by their angelic singing as we laid out the canvas labyrinth on the grass. Several local children gathered to watch and ask us what we were doing. We did our best to explain it to them and realized that any efforts we made to save the experience for the older kids would be futile, as the two- to ten-year-olds were gathering quickly. We instructed them to take off their slippers, roller blades, and tennis shoes and to don a pair of the socks we had brought in an effort to keep the labyrinth clean. Soon the labyrinth was swarming with running, laughing children, as the teens for the youth group began to gather with curiosity.

When the youth group was to begin, we asked the little ones to step aside so the older kids could have a turn. They obediently left the circle of the labyrinth, only to stand patiently on the side, watching and waiting for their turn again, saying, "Auntie? When the big kids are done, can we go again? Can we? Can we?"

The teens formed a circle in the center as I explained the process of the metaphorical pilgrimage to them. They then walked the labyrinth with a solemnity that was a marked contrast to the little ones' playful antics.

After the walk, we sat in a circle to discuss our thoughts and feelings. The younger children came and sat with us, quietly soaking up the "adult" experience. When the older kids moved off to the side to have pizza, a few of the younger ones asked if they could now, finally, have their turn again. This time, rather than running it as a game, the children walked it quietly as they had seen their older brothers and sisters do.

With only two little ones left on the labyrinth—a handsome, four-year-old boy with a shaved head and a beautiful, sparkly-eyed seven-year-old girl—I decided to take my turn as well.

As soon as I had stepped into the labyrinth, Malia, the little girl, came running over from where she had been and began walking immediately behind me. She announced, "I am going to follow you."

I laughed and said, "Okay," taking note to see what emerging metaphors were brewing for me. We had walked silently for about thirty seconds when she asked, "Do you know your way into the lab?" as if it had occurred to her that she might be following the wrong person.

I answered assuredly, "Yes, I know my way."

After maybe another minute of silence, again this sweet girl's voice rose up from behind me, "Are you *sure* you know your way?"

I again assured her I knew what I was doing, but I had to laugh to myself at the metaphor mirror of my own inner child's voice—"Are you sure you know what you are doing?"—which I so often wonder as I wander through life.

When the three of us reached the center, we all sat down crossed-legged and closed our eyes. All choosing to open our eyes at the exact same time, we greeted each other with giggles as we caught each other "peeking." As I looked across the center of the labyrinth at these two beautiful children, I felt as if I was sitting with the childhood version of the Dalai Lama and a young Mary or Holy Mother. Tears came to my eyes as I sat with them, humbled.

Then Malia said, "Okay, close your eyes. Let's listen to God." We all obediently followed her instructions when, only seconds later she added, "Listen for Jesus!"

After several minutes, as the two children got up to walk out, I whispered, "Did you hear God?"

They both smiled and nodded. I asked, "What did he say?"

Malia looked thoughtful as she prepared to leave the center, then answered sweetly, "He said, 'I am always with you!'" She then turned and followed the labyrinth path back out, knowing she was not alone.

⊕ When we allow ourselves silent time, we are able to hear the voice of God.

⊕ When in prayer, instead of just talking to God, listen.

⊕ When you close your eyes and listen, what does God/dess say to you?

7.

TAKE INSPIRED ACTION

A man's heart deviseth the way, but the Lord directeth his steps.
- PROVERBS 41:9

I arrived at the St. John's labyrinth on Maui one evening to prepare for a moonlight labyrinth walk, only to discover two of my friends, a couple, already in the center. After their walk, I asked the man about his experience and he shared that he had been so content in the center he didn't want to leave. When his girlfriend got up to walk back out of the labyrinth, he felt torn between staying in the center and staying with his girlfriend. Reluctantly, he opted to leave with her and began his journey back out.

As he wandered the spiraling path, he suddenly found himself back in the center—somehow he had inadvertently stepped over a line reversing his direction and "losing his way," which caused him to return to the heart of the labyrinth. He laughed as he shared how the labyrinth beautifully mirrored to him the importance of honoring his own pace and his own path while staying within relationships with others.

Many of us can relate to the impulse to ignore our own spiritual yearnings in order to honor the desires of a loved one, or to cater to a relationship or the need to be loved. This often renders us resentful, even though it was our choice. This man's experience was a wonderful reminder to take actions inspired by our core—generated from a state of divine alignment.

Pay careful attention to your own intuition and trust your inner knowing of what is right for you. Our bodies are excellent gauges and will often leave us with a "sinking feeling" in the gut when we aren't supposed to do something and an "all systems go" when we are. By paying attention to these subtleties, we can honor the desires of our spirit. By being authentic, we find that our relationships are benefited, not destroyed, because we bring forth a more honest, joyful self to the relationship.

⊕ **Take action that is inspired by your spirit.**

⊕ **When we act out of our ego-needs rather than from divine alignment, we are likely to make a choice that does not feel right.**

⊕ **Before you take an action, take the time to get centered.**

⊕ **Honor your own heart path!**

8.

PERSEVERE

Spiritual Success comes by understanding the mystery of life;
and by looking on all things cheerfully and courageously,
realizing that events proceed according to a beautiful divine plan.
- PARAMAHANSA YOGANANDA, Scientific Healing Affirmations

ONE OF THE first metaphors I encountered on the labyrinth was the awareness that, as I walked in, within the first few turns I was gratifyingly close to the center. Regardless of whether this "taste" of getting there was a teaser or a false illusion, it left me with a sense of pleasure at how simple this path would be, and how close I was to the goal—even at the outset of the journey.

Before long, however, after encountering turn after turn that took me what seemed like further and further from the goal, I had a sense that I would never reach my destination. I realized that I had been "so close and yet so far."

After a long stretch around the outer rim, I found myself almost right back where I had started, separated from the entrance by only a single line. Thinking I had made no progress at all and would never reach the middle, I ventured on to find that I was only a few short turns from the center.

This part of the walk reflects the concept that "it is darkest just before the dawn." How like life this is! So often we think, "I can do it, no problem," only to encounter challenge after challenge, seemingly taking us further and further away from our goals. Then, just when we think it is useless and we will never succeed at our task, we suddenly find that we are right there, only a moment away from success.

⊕ **Never give up on that which truly matters to you. Just when you think "it" will never happen, or things will never get better, that is often the moment just before everything turns around.**

9.
FIND YOUR PERFECT PACING

To everything there is a season, a time to every purpose under heaven.
~ ECCLESIASTES 3:1

SITTING IN a circle with a group of student government leaders who had just walked the labyrinth, I asked them to share their experiences. One twelve-year-old girl said, "I noticed that I always keep a steady pace as I walk. But what I realized is that sometimes it would serve me better if I were to speed up and sometimes it would serve me better if I were to slow down. A steady pace is not always the best thing for me."

As you walk the labyrinth, or as you go through life, it is important to find a pace that works for you. Often as we walk, we encounter someone in front of us who is walking slower or someone who is on our heels walking faster. As in all relationships, we must find a way to honor our own pace and those of the people with whom we are in relationship. Learning to negotiate these differences is one of life's challenges—and purposes.

One of the beautiful things about relationships is that the others we encounter often can influence us to try life at a different pace. With some people we tend to dance through life, while we opt to carry others. Although it is important to honor your natural pace, it can be exhilarating to try on different paces, styles, and attitudes for size. Allow the labyrinth to be a safe place to "try on" different aspects of your personality. If you always walk slowly, speed up. If you think you must stay between the lines, try walking on the lines to see what that feels like. If you have rules about "right and wrong" ways to walk, try walking the labyrinth the "wrong" way, recognizing that any rules you invent for your labyrinthine journey are your own rules, not "the" rules. Observe the rules you hold yourself to and decide whether or not they are really serving you. Then, consciously choose to live by the "rules" that do.

We are not static beings. We are fluid. We are free to change and grow and run and leap. So often, I hear people say things like, "That's just the way I am, I just have a bad attitude," as if it is unalterable. Spend some time trying out different ways of being. If you have "a bad attitude," try on a good one for a day. S-t-r-e-t-c-h. Break out of your mold and see if you can find your most *authentic* self—not your *automatic* self.

⊕ **What is your natural pace?**

⊕ **In what areas of your life would it serve you better to speed up?**

⊕ **In what areas of your life would it serve you better to slow down?**

⊕ **How do the people you encounter influence your pacing . . . and how do you influence theirs?**

10.
CELEBRATE TRANSITIONS

We are not human beings on a spiritual path, we are spiritual beings on human path.
~ JEAN SHINODA BOLEN

ONCE AS I walked the labyrinth with my parents, we sat in the center together. I felt so joyful and complete to be sharing the experience with them. Then, one after the other, they got up to leave the center before me. Suddenly, I felt so saddened by their leaving, as if the metaphor was that they had died, leaving me there.

Torn, I felt their loss, yet I knew I must stay in the center; it was not my time to go. As I sat there and they moved around me in the labyrinth, I realized that we were still on the same path, just at different stages. I could sense them out there, leading the way.

Our ancestors die and walk the path ahead of us, just as we will walk the path ahead of our children. Regardless of our sequence in this, we remain on the same path, sharing the experience. Death is a *part* of existence, not the *end* of existence. It is simply the part of the journey before we enter the labyrinth again.

My favorite times of day are sunrise and sunset. These are the times of obvious transition. While dealing with change often is the hardest thing we encounter in life, the moments of major transition often are the most beautiful and the most treasured.

In actuality, *every* moment is a moment of transition. Everything around us is in constant flux and change. Nothing remains the same. We cannot step into the same river twice; by the time we place our foot in it again, the water has moved on and the river has changed. By the same token, we cannot encounter the same person twice; between "visits" we change, we learn, we grow, we have new reasons to laugh and new reasons to cry. As the labyrinth pattern illustrates, the only thing that remains unchanging, still, and constant is the sacred core. By coming to know this divine essence within, we are able to anchor in our hearts, to root in love. Remember, the core of the word *emergency* is *emergence*. Embrace life's transitions and allow the new to emerge. Expand the boundary of the labyrinth, the sacred pilgrimage, to include birth, life, and death.

⊕ **Celebrate birth as a time of letting go, a time of preparation.**

⊕ **Celebrate life as a time of illumination.**

⊕ **Celebrate death as a time of union.**

⊕ **Live your life as if you are always in the sacred center.**

11.
RITUALIZE EVERYDAY TASKS

*It is not what we do or how much we do but how much love we put into the actions
because that action is our love for God in action.*
- MOTHER TERESA, *Everything Starts from Prayer*

SOMETIMES WHEN we have a moonlight labyrinth walk on Maui, we have had as many as fifty people at once, poised to walk. With this many people coming and going, it is quite a different experience than when the labyrinth is walked alone or in small groups. I have come to enjoy this added bit of traffic, because I now view all of the activity as a sacred dance rather than as a crowd.

I have applied this metaphor to traffic in a big city, as well. I know this is a stretch, but I have actually been stuck in traffic in the midst of Los Angeles, which I would ordinarily grumble about, when a sudden "shift" of consciousness happened. I have felt myself to be in the midst of an amazing pilgrimage, instead. There we were, thousands and thousands of vehicles all going the same way, in the same place, at the same time of day. What are the chances of that exact combination?

While this may seem unfeasible to those of you who encounter daily traffic battles, rest assured that you can shift your focus to experience anything as an act of devotion to God. As you practice this mindset, it will become easier and easier to achieve, and life's little setbacks will become more tolerable—maybe even joyful—when you choose to see them this way.

- ⊕ Shift your consciousness to make all of your daily activities rituals to honor God and your spiritual path.

- ⊕ What if, while taking a shower, you realized that you were bathing the body of God/dess?

- ⊕ What if, while you were preparing meals or washing dishes, you adopted the mindset that you are serving God?

- ⊕ The tasks don't change, but the enjoyment of them does.

- ⊕ Choose to make every action a devotion!

Part 3

Taking the Pilgrimage Home

Uncommon Sense

People say that walking on water is a miracle, but to me,
walking peacefully on the Earth is the real miracle.
~ THICH NHAT HANH

THE THIRD PART of the pilgrimage journey is taking the insights and guidance you've received back home, where you can apply them in your life. However, as mentioned in the beginning of this book, often when you first observe yourself and your life, you become aware of ideas and feelings but you may not yet know what they mean. Because of this, it is necessary to practice some steps that will allow the fruits of your journey to ripen.

There are several ways you can go about taking the lessons of the labyrinth and the lessons of life to a deeper level. One is to simply live with the idea for a few days and let it bounce around in the back of your mind until it pops out later fully developed. Sometimes an idea will suddenly make sense even a month or two after the experience.

My personal favorite ways come in the process of sharing through writing and talking. Journaling about your insights and *ah-has* is a great way to gain clarity about their meaning and their application in your life. Set aside some regular time to write about all of your thoughts, feelings, and insights. Be careful not to judge or edit, just allow a free flow of words to pour onto the page.

Talking with a friend who is like-minded, one with whom you can share your ideas until they make more sense, also is helpful. Friends, family and fellow pilgrims can reflect back different dimensions of an idea or thought until the concept comes into a clear, full view.

When we take the time to process our experiences, layers of understanding are revealed to us that we could have easily missed. It is often not until we hear ourselves explaining our experience that we understand it, and by sharing our *ah-has* and metaphors we assist others in understanding their own. The greatest challenge is not to dismiss the labyrinth experience at face value if the meaning doesn't come to you right away. Many of the meanings of my own experiences on the labyrinth didn't fully emerge until I processed them on paper. It was then that the pieces of the puzzles started to come together. Remember, we are always on the labyrinth. If the experiences of your life don't make sense to you right away, trust the process, look for the metaphor, and allow the meanings to reveal themselves.

Listen to Your Intuition
*Few is the number of those who think with their own minds
and feel with their own hearts.*
- ALBERT EINSTEIN

INSIGHTS OFTEN emerge when we allow ourselves some quiet time. Meditating, or even just sitting silently on the beach or in your backyard, offers an opportunity to hear the voice of your soul. We each have intuition that guides us, but while we all have this sense in common, what is not common is paying attention to it. Like anything we wish to become good at, it requires practice to develop this skill. The tricky part is that, in our world full of activity and noise and in our brains of constant chatter, it is hard to hear our intuition. Silence is a necessary ingredient for hearing our subtle inner urgings.

And, while the labyrinth is a wonderful tool for accessing our inner wisdom and gaining insights, we can do so even when we are not in the labyrinth. The labyrinth simply allows us an opportunity to become familiar with the voice of our hearts, the voice of God. For some, this will be the first time you've consciously heard the voice of wisdom within. Others may recognize it with a sense of, "Oh, *that* was *you!*" In either case, once we've consciously heard our own intuition, we can then more easily recognize it not only when we are in the labyrinth but also in moments of our daily life when we need it the most.

God is like a composer of beautiful music. When we allow ourselves some silence, our intuition is able to hear that music. The rest of our being is then able to use all of the other gifts we've received—intellect, emotions, talents,

79

feelings, our bodies—to play the music. The labyrinth is an amplifier so we can better hear our intuition. The music is how we choose to live our lives.

In the movie, City of Angels, there is a great scene where all the angels gather on the beach in silence at sunrise and sunset to listen to heavenly music—that no one but they can hear. Imagine if we were to get quiet enough, daily, that we, too, could hear that heavenly music!

⊕ Take time to experience peace daily—not just to pray for it, wish for it, visualize it or judge yourself or others for not having it. Experience it in the moment, now. Sit in silence and simply observe your breathing. Slow it down, make each breath conscious. Then whenever you think of it, stop, breathe, self-observe, let go, breathe, return to heart, return to calm, return to peace. When each of us know how to find peace within, we stand a chance of creating peace in the world.

⊕ As you sit in silence, observe not only your breath moving in and out, but begin to pay attention to the 180-degree turns in your breathing—the turning point from in to out, from out to in. Note the similarity between the route your breath takes and the turns within the labyrinth. Just as traversing the turns within the labyrinth will eventually bring you to the center, simply observing each breath will eventually lead you to your own center, as well.

A MATTER OF PERSPECTIVE

Our scientific power has outrun our spiritual power.
We have guided missiles and misguided men.
~ MARTIN LUTHER KING, JR.

A THIRTEEN-YEAR-OLD girl once came into my office at the school where I was counseling. She wanted to talk about God, religion, witchcraft, and power—touchy subjects in a public school system. She went on to explain to me that she didn't believe in God, but I could see that she was seeking, nonetheless.

Our souls yearn for our egos to get out of the way and allow us to live authentically. This young woman's search to make sense of power and spirit was a sign that she wanted to believe in something greater that she sensed was out there—she just didn't know what to believe. This was the "spiritual indigestion" mentioned earlier—a yearning, a sense, a subtle knowing.

She went on to talk about the devil. I stopped her and said, "Wait a minute. You don't believe in God, but you do believe in the devil?"

She looked at me as if I were totally clueless as only a teenager can, and replied, "I *know* there is a devil because of all the bad things that happen in the world."

I asked, "By that same logic, wouldn't all the good things in the world be evidence of God?"

She couldn't accept this, as if believing in God would require too much rearranging of how she was choosing to live. It's easy to make poor choices if you only believe in the devil. Ultimately, what we choose to believe or not to believe doesn't change *what is* at all. What our beliefs *do* change is *ourselves.* When we believe in or *know* God, we are somehow called to a higher standard of living and require ourselves to make wiser choices—not out of fear of punishment, but rather out of deep respect and love.

We choose to see what we want to see. Unfortunately, she chose to see the bad, but not the good life has to offer. What is good and what is bad is relative, of course. As we mature and evolve, our perspective changes. Often, what we originally think is "bad" is the very thing that changes our lives for the better. With some eventuality, we are able to understand the divine rhyme and reason behind every event.

Acts of a Loving God

There are two forces—gravity and grace. Grace means you are being pulled upward, gravity means you are being pulled downward.
~ OSHO

82

I WAS LOOKING over a contract recently that had a disclaimer section entitled, "Acts of God." It went on to site several instances for which the contract would not be held accountable, including the usual natural disasters: hurricanes, earthquakes, and tidal waves. The statement went on to include war, government regulation, strikes, and civil disorder. When we are in the midst of events such as these, it is easy to see them as "acts of God"—if our God is a vengeful, wrathful God. The challenge we all face is to realize that these events are the acts of a *loving* God.

Even disasters that break our hearts demonstrate to us the perseverance of the human spirit. In the midst of the horror, as we watch the devastation, we see thousands of people banding together to help those in need. Prayer groups pop up all over the world to send blessings to those most immediately effected by the event. People give money and supplies to assist with the rescue and rebuilding efforts. These terrible, "bad" events offer us opportunities to bring out our loving, giving natures.

If there were no sickness, what would Mother Teresa have done with her life to express her goodness? If there were no "bad things," would we be motivated to be thankful for the "good things"? How often has something that you thought was "good" turned out to have a down side—or vice versa?

Event + Response = Outcome[1]

If you were to interview the people who are the social workers of society, you would find that often the reason they got into caring for others was because they had gone through a "bad" experience in their lives during which they needed help. Through their difficult life experiences they gained the necessary

---

1. Event + Response = Outcome was taught to me by Jack Canfield, co-author of the *Chicken Soup for the Soul*® series. For additional information on the powerful application of the equation E+R=O, see Eve Eschner Hogan, *Intellectual Foreplay* (Hunter House, 2000).

insight and compassion to help other people. So, who is to say that what happened to them was really a bad thing? From another perspective, it was a good thing. Good and bad are relative. The inherent goodness or badness isn't in the event, but in our response to it.

Events are simply "what is" and our lives are made up of a lot of them—the things that happen, the things people say, the turns in the road. What makes the result "good or bad" depends on how we respond to the events. Our choices, our responses, are what determine their impact. As the saying goes, "Life is 10 percent what happens to you and 90 percent what you do about it." By walking the labyrinth, we can practice the skills that help us make choices that are in alignment with our divine essence, that are in alignment with the results we want to create. Self-observation helps us not only to see the observer and the observed as different, but also helps us to separate the events from our responses to the events. Then, when we journey back out of the labyrinth, we can take those skills into our lives and create more powerful results.

When a miner goes into a mine looking for gold, he has to remove tons and tons of dirt and rock to find even a single nugget of gold, but he never goes into the mine looking for the dirt. He goes in looking for the gold. As we move through life, we will encounter tons and tons of challenging moments, unpleasant encounters, and difficulties—twists and turns on the path. If we live our lives looking for those things, that is what we will see. If, instead, we live looking for the blessings and opportunities, they are certainly there to be discovered. Amazingly, often we are able to see them as one and the same thing!

Since life is a spiritual journey, everything we encounter on the path is there for the purpose of our growth. The challenge is to learn to travel this journey in divine alignment. Can we shift our perspective and utilize each moment as an opportunity to master our responses? Can we learn not to simply "live through this," but also to *love through it—regardless of what life brings*? Can we journey out of the labyrinth of life with hearts more open and with wiser minds?

If we approach life like a gold miner, a *God* miner, and "go in looking for the God," that, indeed, is what we will find. The same is true as we look at ourselves. We choose whether "gravity pulls us downward or whether grace pulls us upward." The force we are propelled by is not an outside job, it is an internal perspective. The shift from one to the other may not be easy, but it is simple. Simply choose to see everything as a blessing and then watch for the evidence that this is so.

Set Your Sails

RAMAKRISHNA IS quoted as saying, "The breeze of Grace is always blowing, but you must set your sails to catch it." "Setting your sails" begins as a conscious effort, but the more you look for the blessings that are continuously surrounding you, the more easily you will see them. Eventually, with continuous practice, you will be able to see everything as a blessing and offer thanks for it—even before you know what the blessing is.

When we live life from a place of absolute gratitude, everything shifts. Just imagine what life would be like if you were prayerfully thankful for every experience, every opportunity, and every challenge set before you, knowing

85

that it is perfect! Sometimes, the perfection may be simply in the form of an opportunity for you to practice your skills of forgiveness, perseverance, compassion, or understanding. What if all the "turns" in life are really part of the "divine centrifugal force" that moves you toward the center?

I was raised saying a mealtime prayer that speaks to the perspective that everything is a blessing, everything is God, as there is no other thing to be. In the original prayer, the word "Brahmin" was used rather than "God," but because it means the same thing, I've changed the word here to make the language easier to understand.

> *God is the ritual. God is the offering. God is he who offers to the fire that is God. If one sees God in every action, one will find God.*

Translated literally, this prayer is a reminder that not only is God the worship, but God is the flower or incense or love that is offered. God is the one doing the offering and God is the one being offered to. When we shift our perspective so that we see God in everything, every offering, every action, and everyone, we will realize God. We will also recognize our Selves in this prayer.

Again, it is through the process of self-observation, remembering who you are, letting go of who you aren't, and aligning with your divine self that you are able to shift your perspective and thus, your life, to embody this concept.

When we encounter experiences on the labyrinth—memories, judgments, thoughts, people—they are merely metaphors to help us see what we need to see, let go of what we need to release, and remember what we need to know so that we can experience a union with the Divine. *The same holds true outside of the labyrinth.*

WALKING THE HEART PATH EVERY DAY

The one purpose of human life is to attain devotion to God and
spiritual illumination; otherwise, life is meaningless.
~ SWAMI PRABHAVANANDA

WHEN WALKING the labyrinth, it is easy to see that the different experiences we have are metaphors for what we need to see about ourselves. When we have judgments about others within the labyrinth, we can learn to look at ourselves and recognize that we are being given the opportunity to realign. Then we can release the judgment, return to our hearts, and "allow" others the room to walk their own paths in their own ways.

When we are pilgrims on a designated sacred journey, it is much easier to maintain the awareness that the other people we encounter are also pilgrims. From this perspective, when something happens that might cause us to pass judgment, we can more easily remember that one of the reasons we are on this journey is to return to our hearts and to be more loving. Hence, forgiveness, understanding, and compassion are more readily available. The challenging task for each of us is applying these same skills outside of the labyrinth or once we have returned home from the pilgrimage—in our lives, when we don't have the step-by-step reminder of who we are and where we are—on a sacred path.

In order to walk your heart path on a daily basis, you must set your intention regularly. Observe yourself, remember who you are, and align your actions with your heart.

⊕ **Take some time to evaluate just what your heart path looks like. What are the qualities you choose to embody? What kind of friends do you choose to have? What kind of relationships are you in? How do you choose to spend your time? What kind of impact will you have while you are here? How do you want to be remembered? What will people say about you? What do you value? What do you believe in? What do you care about? What do you intend to do, and how do you choose to be?**

⊕ **Let your mind dwell on some holy personality—Christ, Muhammad, Buddha, Mary, Mother Teresa—your choice. Then concentrate your mind upon his/her heart. Try to imagine what it must feel like to be a great saint—pure and untroubled by the way of the world, a knower of God. Most of us have heard the popular saying "What would Jesus do?" Rather than pondering what the saint you are dwelling on would do, feel that the saint's heart has become your heart within your own body. Feel with his/her heart. Observe how you feel as your heart and his/her heart beat as one. Become familiar with this feeling and know you can return to it. Then, as you are feeling the holy heartbeat within, ask yourself, "What would *I* do? What would *love* do?" Then, align your actions.**

What Are Your Charms?

SEVERAL YEARS ago my husband and I decided we wanted to buy a home in a really nice part of Maui. The house we chose was all glass and wood and had a beautiful ocean view. We set our hearts on buying this house, but there was one problem. We didn't have enough money for a house of that magnitude. Consequently, we did what all young people do who want something they can't afford—we called mom and dad.

Of course, my parents were not terribly impressed with the idea of us buying a house that was so far out of our financial league. Unbeknownst to me, after we hung up the phone, my parents spoke with a swami in India who is a dear friend of our family and shared their concerns about what I wanted to do. That night I had the most amazing dream.

I dreamt that I was sitting in this swami's office in India, he on one side of his desk and I on the other. The overhead fan rattled in a vain attempt at cooling the humid Indian air. After looking into my eyes—and I suspected into my heart as well—he quietly said, "I want to show you something." He rose from his chair while I ventured toward him, meeting him halfway.

He gently lifted his coral-colored robes to expose his ankles and waited for me to pay full attention. Beautiful gold and jewel-encrusted charm anklets hung on each leg. Gasping slightly, both in surprise and in delight, I looked up, seeking an explanation.

Somewhat matter-of-factly, as if everyone should have anklets of this splendor, he explained, "Each of these charms represents a spiritual moment in my life or a special connection I have shared with another human being."

89

He proceeded to show me the charm that represented my place in his life and the ones for each of my family members, who were also family to him after forty years of a heartfelt association. He then simply let me examine the intricacy and beauty of each charm. As if they had somehow captured the emotion, just gazing at each evoked the feelings that were generated by the original event or relationship they symbolized.

He then said, "Now let us see what is on *your* ankles," emphasizing "your" in such a way that I sensed what was to come was not going to hold a candle to what he was showing me.

Curious to see myself, hoping to see similar charms of gold, I lifted my skirt, only to discover a shiny, multicolored plastic band on each ankle, the kind they pass out at resorts on Maui to identify you as a guest. Shocked and disappointed, I looked closer and discovered that printed on the sparkly plastic band was the address of the house I was trying to buy.

I had an instant understanding that if I were to continue on my current path and buy the house, I would not have time for magical moments in nature or intimate encounters with others, because I would be too busy trying to keep my "resort." With one last glimpse into the holy man's eyes, I woke from my dream, crying.

Needless to say, we opted not to buy that house but settled instead for one that was more affordable. Since that dream, however, I have had cause to consider just exactly what I choose to have on my "anklets."

In many cultures, anklets represent our ties to the earth. Some jingle when we walk to remind us of God with each step, others are symbolic of our purpose or intention. In the case of my dream, the charms were gathered, or perhaps earned, with the recognition of each heart-touching moment.

⊕ What if we were to live our lives as if we were here to "collect holy charms"? What kinds of heart connections are you making? Think about your life as it is now. What kinds of charms do you have on your anklets so far? What are your magic moments? Think of the different people in your life. If you were to put a symbol on a charm for each relationship, what would the charms look like? If you were to string all of the charms together, would there be a common theme? Do you like what you see? Do you want to show your anklets, or keep them hidden from others' view?

⊕ If you were to begin your "charmed life" now, what kind of charms or symbols would you like to represent your life?

⊕ Magic moments and heart connections stem from experiences of compassion, love, and appreciation. What if you were to live as if each encounter was one deserving of a heart connection? How would you behave differently?

91

Simple Steps

I WORKED for years as a counselor in an intermediate school, working with children who were at an age notorious for being challenging. Sometimes, when I was looking at a class of these adolescents, I imagined that each of them was God—in camouflage. As I did this, I imagined that this was a game of divine hide and seek, and my job was to see God, to see the good, in each of them. If for no other reason, it makes the routine of our daily tasks more fun and challenging. However, if practiced, it can become a skill that will transform the way you see the world.

⊕ **Start with seeing God in children—it is easiest to see past the disguise in them. Then move up through the ages. The better you get at this, the more challenging the game can become. Imagine that all the people you work with, all the people you encounter throughout your day, are God in disguise. Your challenge is to see beyond the camouflage to the glimmer of light within, to see their creativity, their talents, their loving natures. Your job is to be a miner who looks for the gold, not the dirt. You'll be amazed at how much fun this is. You will also laugh heartily at some of the costumes God tries to hide in. Just like a computer game, once you've mastered the beginner levels, try moving into the advanced. Learn to love the "unlovable." Learn to love your "enemies." Of course, the most advanced level is to look in the mirror, deeply into your own eyes, and see God within.**

⊕ **Another great exercise for experiencing heart connections is to make a habit of blessing people as you pass by. Think about how often we have judgments about other people—how they are driving, what they are wearing, what they are doing. Remember, these judgements are really stemming from our heart's desire to love, but it is showing up as an ego-need to control. Imagine that instead of judging people,**

you send them a prayer or a blessing. Pray for the person driving poorly. Pray for the person who is challenged mentally or physically. Pray for the person who irritates you the most. Not only will you be contributing to their well-being, you will find that it truly is in the giving that we receive. It feels good to send loving energy out into the world, and you will discover that it finds its way back home. Love knows the path by heart.

This is along the same lines as the "Practice Random Acts of Kindness" campaign, in which people are encouraged to go out into the world and do kind things with no expectation of return. In addition to kindness, practice conscious acts of compassion. Take a moment to imagine how you would feel in another's shoes and treat that person as you would like to be treated—from the perspective of being a *spiritual being*.

We've all heard the Golden Rule: Do unto others as you would have them do unto you. The catch is that the rule only works if we are in a state of re-membrance that we are divine and deserve to be treated as such—and so do others. As the Dalai Lama points out, "If we do not love ourselves, how can we love others?" If you think you are a sinner, it's easy to think that others have a right to mistreat you—and that you, therefore, have a right to mistreat them. If you think you are a sinner, it seems only natural to sin. If, instead, you know you are divine, and so are those you encounter, you will be more likely to treat one another with love and respect. If your true nature is divine, made in the image and likeness of God, then it is only natural to behave as such.

So often, we operate on automatic pilot in terms of how we treat others. We say sarcastic things or little barbs in an unskilled attempt to get them to comply. None of us likes to be treated that way, yet we so easily slip into doing it to others—especially to children, who are not in a position of sticking up for themselves. They then, in turn, treat one another poorly and the ripple effect of put-downs generates outward. If the words or behaviors are not appropriate to be said or done on your spiritual path or pilgrimage, they are not appropriate for your spiritual journey through life. Be the stone that is thrown into the pond of humankind, and be the source of a ripple of goodness that is never-ending!

Become an Instrument of Peace

Lord, make me an instrument of thy peace.
Where there is hatred, let me sow love.
Where there is injury, pardon.
Where there is doubt, faith.
Where there is despair, hope.
Where there is darkness, light.
Where there is sadness, joy.

Oh Divine Master, grant that I may not so much seek to be consoled as to console,
to be understood as to understand,
to be loved as to love.
For it is in giving that we receive,
it is in pardoning that we are pardoned,
and it is in dying that we are born to eternal life.
- ST. FRANCIS

IN EVERY field of work you will encounter people who are instruments of peace. These are the people who do the little things that make a difference in your day. They are the ones whose disguise is a little easier to see through. It might be the grocery clerk at the market taking time to ask how you are doing, it might be a nurse, a paperboy, a waitress, or a teacher with a warm smile or kind words. It doesn't matter what they do, what matters is who they are, how they treat others, and how they approach life.

Instruments of peace are like "social ministers," of sorts. They are the people who are actually out in the world, loving people into a better situation as they walk their own personal winding paths. They look for the good—

reaching in with both hands to pull the newborn out of us, to release our inner spirits and our inner joys.

My friend Jane is an ultrasound technician who scans people's ailments daily. Even after more than twenty years, she makes a game out of helping stressed and worried people to feel better, stronger, and more in control of their lives. Recently, she scanned a lady who was very upset and nervous. The doctor called Jane to say that the patient needed to have a blood sample drawn. He told her to send the patient back to him to do it because, based on past history, he thought the patient would pass out.

Rather than buying into the fragility of the patient, Jane opted to help this woman identify with her capable, strong, centered self, rather than her fearful, weak self. She took some time to speak to the woman as she scanned her, telling her how strong she looked and how capable of handling the tests she was.

Jane told her, "The doctor thinks I need to send you back to him to do the blood work, but I am sure you can do it here. You are so much stronger than you know!"

By the time Jane was through, the woman successfully had her blood drawn and, rather than leaving the hospital an emotional wreck, she walked out feeling ready to handle whatever came her way. This was the act of an instrument of peace.

⊕ **Aim to make your relationships with people—loved ones and strangers alike—encounters they will never forget rather than those they will never get over. As instruments of peace, it is our job to stop, self-observe, and remember not only who we are but also** *who the other person is*—and to choose our actions from there. Make life a game to see how many people you can powerfully impact in an unforgettable and wonderful way.

Train Your Brain to Start With Heart

PRACTICING ACTS of compassion is what it means to walk your heart path every day. Thus, you must train your brain to start with heart! When we are coming from our hearts, we are able to use our heads and make choices that will be in the best interests of all involved. We must no longer react from automatic pilot when we work with other people—most especially our young ones and our loved ones—but instead choose words and actions that are in alignment with our intent, to replace doubt with faith, hatred with love, and sadness with joy.

⊕ **Practice giving thanks. Many of us are familiar with the concept of saying thanks in grace before a meal. Extend this consciousness to say thank you for everything. Try for a day, or even just an hour, to offer thanks to God for everything that happens. Say thank you for the parking spot you receive—no matter how far away from your destination. Say thank you for the ability to walk across the lot. Say thank you for the opportunity to practice forgiveness and letting go. Say thank you for the challenges and the obvious blessings. Say thank you for every expression of love. Say thank you for every encounter with another human being—then aim to make it an encounter they will be thankful for as well. Look for things to be thankful for.**

⊕ Use your prayer time as an opportunity to give thanks, instead of an opportunity to ask for something. The more you become thankful for, the more you will see what you already have and the less you will need to ask for anything.

⊕ Turn every moment, every action into an offering of devotion. When I was twenty-one, I took care of my ninety-four-year-old, bedridden grandmother. Because she needed twenty-four-hour care, this was not an easy task. Sometimes it became so difficult that I cried and wanted to give up. Then I started consciously "pretending" that my grandmother was God in disguise, and that my job was to maintain an attitude of serving God in Grandma. By shifting this view of my grandmother, I was able to turn daily tasks—vacuuming, cleaning, and personal care—into a spiritual opportunity. What if we were to do all of the same things we already do, but change the attitude with which we do them? How would your life be different?

Moment to Moment, Step by Step

Now we are no longer separated from our source, and behold,
we are the source and the source is us. We are so intimately united with Him,
we cannot by any means be separated from Him for we are Him.
- ABRAHAM ABULAFIA

AS YOU walk the labyrinth or take a pilgrimage, you will become aware that you reach your goal by taking one step at a time. The entire experience is made up of one moment after the next. If we align our steps with our goals, we will eventually reach our sacred destination.

Each day is made up of minutes. Each minute is made up of seconds. Your life is made up of moments, moments filled with daily tasks, people, activities, ideas, and feelings. There are times when it's easy to feel like we are not in any semblance of control over what our lives are filled with, but that isn't true. We are. We are faced with choices every moment of every day. We choose which path we walk. We choose whether our lives are filled with soap-opera drama, emotional and physical violence, and out-of-control energy, or whether we walk a path that is filled with magical moments and heartfelt connections. We choose whether to see the dirt or the gold.

Every moment contains the opportunity of choice. When you take a minute to self-observe and suddenly realize that you are not on the path you want to be on, you can make a choice that brings you back to your heart path. You can, in any given moment, make a choice filled with compassion, or a lack thereof. You can make a choice that is resourceful, or not. You can make a choice that is in alignment with your heart, or not. It is up to you.

99

Life is a reflection of your choices. If you don't like what it is showing you, choose differently. Remember that making this change may take a few attempts. The key is not to give up.

When I was eleven, I decided to become a vegetarian, declaring that I would never eat meat again. Two weeks later, I was sitting with my girlfriend while she ate a big, juicy hamburger. I said, "That looks really good. Can I have a bite?" It wasn't until I had swallowed that I remembered I didn't eat meat anymore.

Bringing about change is much like this. We set our intentions and aim to achieve them, then we realize—right after we've "swallowed the bite"—that we've headed off target. Our task then is to once again set our intention. Next time, we may realize in "mid-chew," but we are already committed to our action. We set our intentions again. The next time, we remember just before we "take the bite" and choose to do something different. With a little more practice, we don't even want to "eat a hamburger." This is how change comes about. What if, instead of resetting my intentions, I had said after swallowing the hamburger, "Well, I guess it is hopeless. I knew I couldn't do it"? Change comes about through aligning—and realigning—our actions.

100

⊕ Persevere. Don't give up. Set and reset your intentions. Just when you think you are as far away as you can possibly get, you'll find the path turns and delivers you to the center or returns you home.

⊕ When the grass looks greener on the other side of the fence, water your lawn! Take responsibility for your *ability* to *respond*. You are the creator of your experiences. Your thoughts create your feelings.

Your choices have led you to where you are now and new choices can lead you to a new destination. Observe your "side of the fence" and nourish growth.

✛ **Watch for metaphors. The universe will, literally, give you signs that you are on the right path—or not—if you simply are aware of the messages you receive through metaphor.**

One day I was reading and came across a passage that said, "Hold on to the pillar. Then you can go round and round and there is no fear of falling. That pillar is God."[2] Something about the idea of holding onto the pillar of God for strength appealed me so I stopped to ponder it for a while. Then later that day, I was doing an errand at the boat harbor and realized that I was standing right next to a sign pole as I waited for the boat to come in. Thinking again of the passage I had read, I reached out and grabbed a "hold of the pillar" as a personal symbolic gesture. Then, knowing that everything is metaphor, I decided to look up to see what the sign I had grabbed onto said to see if it metaphorically held a message for me. I was delighted as I read, "Do not leave your vessel unattended." I laughed as I received such excellent advice from the universe! Indeed, when you have a hold on the pillar of God, your vessel is never left unattended!

101

2. Swami Premananda, quoted in *How to Know God: The Yoga Aphorisms of Patanjali*, by Swami Prabhavananda (Vedanta Press, 1996).

There's No Place Like Home

*Though temples may serve as aids to the beginner, they are but symbols of
God's greatest of all temples, the human heart.*
~ SWAMI PRABHAVANANDA

I HAVE BEEN drawn to the idea of taking pilgrimages ever since my first
Cultural Anthropology class, when I heard of the efforts people make to show
their devotion to God. Right then and there, sitting in the classroom, I was
determined to take a pilgrimage.

Since then, I have taken several personal pilgrimages. My sister and I
journeyed to England to seek out Stonehenge and then went on to France to
search for Black Madonnas. We coined this part of the journey "the Madonna
tour" as we walked miles across the countryside, singing spiritual songs, to
places of pilgrimage that promised a statue of a Black Madonna. This particular mission even led us to the Chartres Cathedral, but, unfortunately, it was
before I knew about the labyrinth the cathedral contained. We were there to
kiss the Black Madonna that lies below the labyrinth in the Crypt.

Fortunately, after learning about the labyrinth, I was able to return to Chartres to walk the ancient path of prayer. I was struck by the beauty of the stone work and could feel the devotion emanating from the labyrinth, devotion that was displayed not only by the artists who created this masterpiece, but also from 800 years of pilgrims walking the sacred path.

I also journeyed with my parents to India as a form of pilgrimage in and of itself; in addition, we walked into the Himalayas to an elevation of 11,000 feet to reach a sacred temple. As I walked, I felt as if trekking up the mountain was easy, as if I was being assisted by angel wings; grace was pulling me upward. When we reached the summit, the sky was completely shrouded with a foggy mist. Surrounded by fog, the temple was interesting, but it lacked the splendor one might expect to find at the end of such a journey. (There are those pesky expectations again!) I found myself wondering what the "big deal" was about this particular place, and why they chose to build a temple there.

The next morning, however, as we prepared to enter the temple, the mists suddenly parted just behind the temple to reveal a breathtaking vista of looming, snow-covered Himalayan peaks as a majestic backdrop. This little temple was sitting in a valley, surrounded by God's magnificence. When the veil lifted, for only a few moments, we were offered a glimpse of the immensity of God's blessings, and we instantly knew why we had come. As quickly as it opened, the veil once again filled in, leaving before us only the daily tasks at hand.

This pilgrimage experience also can be looked at metaphorically. So often in life we can only see that which is right before us and we don't recognize that just beyond the veil is an immensity of infinite love, beauty, and wisdom that is

shrouded from us most of the time. If we were able to see it, we would be paralyzed by its wonder and unable to attend to our tasks—the tasks of physical
survival. Those little moments, the magical moments when the shroud of fog
is lifted, are the ones that reach into our hearts and wake our souls, reminding
us of who we are and why we are here.

105

Nighttime represents this same lifting of the veil. It is then that we are
treated to the opportunity to see beyond, to stretch our imaginations and
wonder about eternity and infinity. Whole galaxies are revealed to us that, if
we believed only that which we could see in the daytime, we wouldn't even

know existed. Then, as daylight comes, the stars—that are always there—disappear, allowing us to return to the tasks most immediately before us. But gnawing at the back of our minds is that knowing that there is more to all this than meets the eye. We are in the midst of mystery and wonder.

If we transform our daily tasks into daily acts of devotion, if we see the metaphorical messages that surround us and acknowledge the blessings that are constantly bestowed upon us, we can bring about a state of consciousness that can see through the veil. This enables us to enjoy the immense vista of divine beauty. With this, we stop *seeking* and begin *seeing*. When we are able to see through the veil, to know the infinite well of love that lies within everything and everyone, we can live life with true joy. We no longer need to seek out a pilgrimage, because we know we are already on one.

As Dorothy said so eloquently in *The Wizard of Oz*, "There's no place like home. There's no place like home." While pilgrimages are powerful experiences, we must bring our gifts home so that we can share them with others and put them to use. The Scarecrow had to bring his brains home to apply his newly discovered intelligence. The Lion had to return to the forest to use his courage, and the Tin Man had to follow his newfound heart home. When Dorothy returned to Kansas, she saw her life differently. She felt more love and appreciation for the people in her life and for the multitude of gifts that surrounded her. *This is what we are also called upon to do.*

A Map at the Tips of Your Fingers
When you were born, you cried and the world rejoiced.
Live your life in such a way that when you die, the world cries and you rejoice.
- INDIAN PROVERB

IF YOU don't have access to a labyrinth to walk, merely look to the prints on the tips of your fingers for a reminder of who you are and why you are here. There you will find a labyrinthine map that is uniquely and specifically your very own. No one, in all the billions of people on Earth, has the exact blueprint, exact purpose, exact make-up that you do.

These mini-labyrinth prints are left on everything that you touch. Fingerprints stay there for many, many years—just as everyone you encounter is affected by your presence. While your footsteps—what you do—will disappear in a short time; who you are, how you touch others, lasts for a very, very long time. Know that the effect of the words you say, the thoughts you think, the actions you take, impact the world in a unique way for many years to come. Make your everlasting impact one that's in alignment with your heart.

Our lives are a labyrinthine journey. If we take a moment to self-remember, self-observe, and align our actions with our spirits, no matter which way the winding path turns, it always brings us back home, to love.

Our task is to keep the experience of the pilgrimage alive, to make our homes our temples, to make our lives our worship, to make every action our devotion, to be instruments of peace. This is the way of the winding path.

107

Appendix

Guidelines for Walking the Labyrinth

The 11-cirucit labyrinth, a replica from the Chartres Cathedral in France, is not to be confused with a maze. While mazes are designed to trick you with dead ends and false paths, the labyrinth has only one path leading into the center and the same path leads back out. Rather than a game, the labyrinth offers a metaphorical pilgrimage—a walking meditation.

1. Just like a pilgrimage, the labyrinth offers a three-fold path:

1) **The walk into the labyrinth, representing self-observation and release. This is a time for contemplating your life and letting go of stress, grief, thoughts, and feelings in preparation for reaching the center.**

2) **The center—the sacred destination represents illumination, and is a time for silent meditation. Stay in the center as long as you like, until you feel complete.**

3) **The return journey back out—represents union with God and offers a time for integration in which we take the insights that we gained on the labyrinth into our lives for implementation.**

The magic of the labyrinth walk happens with metaphor. Be self-observant as you walk. The labyrinth will mirror to you what you need to see. Whatever you experience on the labyrinth will offer you insight as to what you need to pay attention to, and perhaps amend, in your life. Everything is metaphor.

2. Guidelines for Walking the Labyrinth:

1. **Let go of expectations.** The message of the labyrinth is often subtle. Just relax and enjoy this peaceful path of prayer.

2. **Be Self-observant.** Pay attention to what you experience as you walk. Be the observed and the observer.

3. **Find your own pace.** Some people will want to walk swiftly, others will walk slowly. Some will run, others will dance.

4. **It is okay to pass.** Utilize the 180-degree turns to step off the path to let someone pass, or to maneuver around someone who is walking more slowly ahead of you.

5. **The labyrinth is a two-way street,** meaning that those who have already reached the center will be coming out as you go in. Simply pay attention to where you are on the labyrinth, step aside, resume your position and continue on your way.

6. **Emotions may be evoked,** simply breathe and observe. Remember that everything is metaphor and the labyrinth will mirror for you anything you need to see.

3. Five Steps to Divine Alignment

In any given moment in which you feel disconnected,
take these simple steps on your heart path.

1. **Self-Remember**

   Remember who you really are. Look to the labyrinth to remind you—it has a calm, still center in the midst of the chaos. The heart of the labyrinth is unwavering, just like your spirit. When you forget who you are, look to small children. All the beautiful qualities they possess, we possess, too: enthusiasm, joy, energy, creativity, imagination, curiosity, playfulness, honesty, authentic self-expression. None of these qualities go away as we grow up, access simply gets blocked. By remembering who you really are, you are beginning to forge the path to your heart.

2. **Self-Observe**

   In order to access your true essence, your inner wisdom, your powerful, purposeful and passionate self, you must be aware of the things that get in the way so that you can choose to remove them. Practice self-observation in every moment of every day. Practice self-observation with each step, each word, each thought and each action. As you do, you will become aware of what you say, think and do—and aware of what serves you and what doesn't. Ask yourself, "Does this diminish or enhance the obstacles to enlightenment?" If your choices enhance the obstacles, then it is time to make new choices.

3. **Letting Go**

   As you encounter the behaviors, thoughts and words that are not serving you, that are blocking access to your heart, take a deep breath and let them go. Breathe and let go. Breathe and let go. You will find that your need for love and your need to be loved are blocking your ability to be loving and to be loved. When encountering obstacles (the things that don't feel good) ask yourself, "Is this my need for approval or my need for control that is getting in my way?" Once you identify one need, the other or both, breathe and let go, breathe and let go. This will take you directly to your heart, to love.

4. **Getting Centered**

   When we are in our heads, we are cut off from our hearts. When we are in our hearts, we can use our heads. Every time you stop to self-remember, self-observe, let go, and get centered you have successfully journeyed from head to heart and have reestablished access. You are now able to be resourceful, re-Source-ful, once-again-full-of-Source. Breathe, replenish, reconnect. When we are resourceful, a multitude of new options and resources become obvious, available and accessible.

5. **Take Aligned Action**

   From your center, you will be empowered to make choices in alignment with who you really are, authentically and enthusiastically. (Enthusiasm, en Theo, in God.) When your thoughts, words, and actions are aligned with who you really are, you are living in divine alignment. You will no longer seek your spiritual path, you will see that this is your spiritual path. Your relationships will improve, your joy will return, your energy, creativity, wisdom, compassion, playfulness, curiosity, life purpose and passion will all be accessible once again.

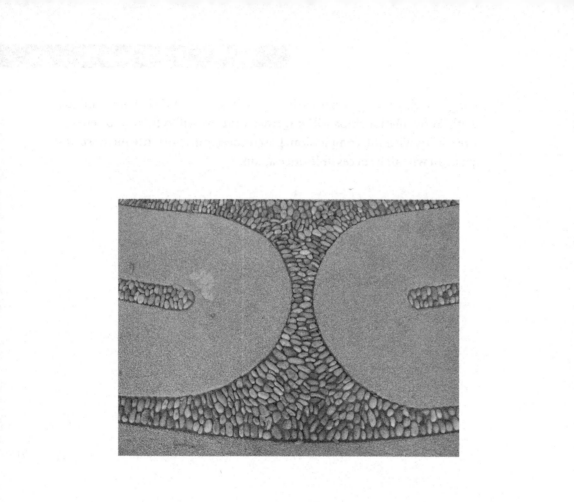

RESOURCES

Labyrinth:

Artress, Lauren, *Walking a Sacred Path,* Riverhead Books, 1995

Geoffrion, Rev. Jill Kimberly Harwell, *Living the Labyrinth: 101 Paths to a Deeper Connection with the Sacred*, Pilgrim Press, 2000.

Lonegren, Sig, *Labyrinths: Ancient Myths and Modern Uses,* Sterling Publications, 2001

Letting Go:

Britt, Jim, with Eve Eschner Hogan, *Rings of Truth*. Health Communications Inc., 1999.

Intuition:

Capacchione, Lucia, *The Power of Your Other Hand,* Newcastle Publishing, 1988

Scalese, Stephen, *The Whisper in Your Heart,* One Spirit One World, 2000

Metaphor:

Cohen, Alan, *A Deep Breath of Life,* Hay House, 1996

Rushnell, Squire, *When God Winks,* Beyond Words Publishing, 2001

Self-Observation:

Perl, Fritz, *The Gestalt Approach,* Science & Behavior Books, 1973

Other Resources:

Cooper, Rabbi David A., *God is a Verb,* Riverhead Books, 1997

Hislop, John, *Conversations with Sathya Sai Baba,* Birth Day Publishing, 1978

Kornfield, Jack, *Buddha's Little Instruction Book,* Bantam Books, 1994

Mother Teresa, *Everything Starts with Prayer*, White Cloud Press, 1998

Osho, *The Book of Secrets*, St. Martin's Griffin, 1974

Prabhavananda, Swami, *The Eternal Companion*, Vedanta Press, 1960

Prabhavananda, Swami, *How to Know God*, Mentor: New American Library, 1953

Ruiz, Don Miguel, *The Four Agreements*, Amber-Allen Publishing, 1997

Yogananda, Paramhansa, *Scientific Healing Affirmations*, Self-realization Fellowship, 1962

Web Sites:

Looking for a Labyrinth in Your Neighborhood? Grace Cathedral's Web Site offers a Labyrinth Locator. www.GraceCathedral.org

Join the Labyrinth Society! A multitude of labyrinth resources await you on this site. www.labyrinthsociety.org

Labyrinth resources, information, and products thoughtfully offered for your personal journey by John Ridder. www.PaxWorks.com

Beautiful web site and resource for Rebecca Rodriguez' Labyrinth Inspiration Cards. www.surrendertotheheart.com/labyrinth.htm

Robert Ferre's Website offers an excellent resource for labyrinth enthusiasts and those desiring a portable canvas labyrinth. www.labyrinthproject.com

Jeff Saward's site is another wonderful resource and home of the Caerdroia Journal of Mazes and Labyrinths. www.labyrinthos.net

Rancho La Puerta is home of the beautiful stone labyrinth shone throughout this book and is truly heaven on Earth. www.rancholapuerta.com

Acknowledgments

SPECIAL THANKS to Berny Dohrmann for introducing me to the labyrinth so sweetly through the gift of a book. Your wisdom and inner guidance brought me to the perfect experiential tool for my life's work!

Sincere appreciation to Reverend Heather Mueller-Fitch of St. John's Church in Keokea, Maui for believing in me from the first moment we met. You were—and continue to be—an answer to my prayers. Sharing monthly moonlight walks with you is pure joy.

Dr. Lauren Artress, thank you for forging the path so beautifully. Your book, *Walking a Sacred Path*, was my first introduction to the labyrinth. Something about the labyrinth grabbed hold of me as I read and I knew my life would never be the same.

Mom and Dad, love, creativity, and true spirituality are caught, not taught. Thank you for such great modeling of living in divine alignment, loving unconditionally and seeing God everywhere. "Thou art my loving mother and compassionate father."

Lauralyn, your continuous belief, trust, generosity and friendship make life so much more wonderful! My labyrinthine work could not have happened without your support. "Thou art my true friend and constant companion."

Thanks to Helen Curry, Sig Lonegren, Jeff Saward, Robert Ferre, David Gallagher, John Ridder, Rev. Jill Geoffrion and the rest of the Labyrinth Society for your help, input, encouragement and most importantly for leading the way!

117

Michael Abbey, thank you for your amazing creative talent as a designer and your generous assistance in designing the cover.

Ana Hays, thanks for joining my team as both publicist and friend, and sharing your talent, insight and heart on the journey!

Jane Foley, thank you for walking the winding publishing path and holding my hand when I needed it. You are a great friend. Bless you!

Steve, thank you for your willingness to accept my venturing into places unknown to see what lies around the next turn in the path. Your support, faith, trust and love overwhelm me. I'm blessed to share life's path with you.

Steven Scholl of White Cloud Press, bless you for getting it from the very beginning! Thank you for your insight, wisdom, loving heart, and friendship.

To my Gurus, thank you for the continuous blessings, guidance and constant presence in my heart. I am humbled to be so blessed!

CPSIA information can be obtained
at www.ICGtesting.com
Printed in the USA
LVOW04n1309021117
553944LV00001BA/1/P

EVE ESCHNER HOGAN is an inspirational speaker and labyrinth facilitator. In addition to *Way of the Winding Path*, she is the creator of the *Spiral Labyrinth Calendar* and the author of "*Intellectual Foreplay*," "*Virtual Foreplay*," co-author of the novel, "*Rings of Truth*," "*Chicken Soup for the Music Lover's Soul*" and senior editor for "*Chicken Soup for the African American Soul*." Eve serves as relationship advisor for DreamMates.com.

Eve holds a Bachelor of Arts degree in Cultural Anthropology, a teaching credential, and a Master's degree in Confluent Education. She also has been honored with a Doctor of Divinity degree and is currently working on a Ph.d. in Transpersonal Psychology.

Founder of *Wings to Wisdom: Tools for Self-Mastery*, Eve facilitates personal and spiritual growth workshops, including labyrinth walks, and performs labyrinth weddings. She possesses a rare and deep understanding of human behavior and is a true example of the principles she shares. Her charismatic style captivates listeners, igniting people's enthusiasm and joy for life.

Her special interest is in helping people discover their own inner resources, thus expanding their strengths and life skills. She leaves her audiences empowered with the skills to effect positive change in their lives.

For information about Eve Eschner Hogan, her workshops, books and calendars: Wings to Wisdom: Tools for Self-Mastery, P.O. Box 943, Puunene, Maui, HI 96784 (808) 879-8648/ Fax: (808) 879-8201

Email:Eve@HeartPath.com   Web: http://www.HeartPath.com